KIDEX for
Infants

Practicing Competent Child Care for Infants

R. Adrienne Boyd, R.N., B.S.N.

THOMSON

DELMAR LEARNING

Australia Canada Mexico Singapore Spain United Kingdom United States

THOMSON

™

DELMAR LEARNING

KIDEX for Infants: Practicing Competent Child Care for Infants
R. Adrienne Boyd, R.N., B.S.N.

Vice President, Career Education SBU:
Dawn Gerrain

Director of Editorial:
Sherry Gomoll

Senior Acquisitions Editor:
Erin O'Connor

Associate Editor:
Chris Shortt

Developmental Editor:
Patricia Osborn

Director of Production:
Wendy A. Troeger

Production Manager:
J.P. Henkel

Production Editor:
Amber Leith

Technology Project Manager:
Sandy Charette

Editorial Assistant:
Stephanie Kelly

Director of Marketing:
Wendy E. Mapstone

Channel Manager:
Kristin McNary

Cover Design:
Joseph Villanova

Composition:
Pre-Press Company, Inc.

For permission to use material from this text or product, submit a request online at
http://www.thomsonrights.com

Any additional questions about permissions can be submitted by email to thomsonrights@thomson.com

Library of Congress Cataloging-in-Publication Data

Boyd, R. Adrienne.
Kidex for infants : practicing competent child care for infants / R. Adrienne Boyd.
      p. cm.
Includes bibliographical references and index.
ISBN-10 1-4180-1270-X (alk. paper)
ISBN-13 978-1-4180-1270-0
1. Day care centers--Administration. 2. Infants--Care.
I. Title.
HQ778.5.B689 2006
362.71'2--dc22

2005023633

NOTICE TO THE READER

Publisher does not warrant or guarantee any of the products described herein or perform any independent analysis in connection with any of the product information contained herein. Publisher does not assume, and expressly disclaims, any obligation to obtain and include information other than that provided to it by the manufacturer.

The reader is expressly warned to consider and adopt all safety precautions that might be indicated by the activities herein and to avoid all potential hazards. By following the instructions contained herein, the reader willingly assumes all risks in connection with such instructions.

The Publisher makes no representation or warranties of any kind, including but not limited to, the warranties of fitness for particular purpose or merchantability, nor are any such representations implied with respect to the material set forth herein, and the publisher takes no responsibility with respect to such material. The publisher shall not be liable for any special, consequential, or exemplary damages resulting, in whole or part, from the readers' use of, or reliance upon, this material.

The authors and Thomson Delmar Learning affirm that the Web site URLs referenced herein were accurate at the time of printing. However, due to the fluid nature of the Internet, we cannot guarantee their accuracy for the life of the edition.

Contents

Preface

INTRODUCTION

KIDEX for Infants is a proven management tool and essential resource for all child care personnel. It is one of a five-part series that includes KIDEX for infants, one-year-olds, two-year-olds, three-year-olds, and four-year-olds. To assist in providing for competent infant care, *KIDEX for Infants* provides helpful information for start-up and existing programs. To accommodate all the demands of creating a well-planned environment while ensuring children are receiving the best possible care, time-saving suggestions are extremely important. This book provides easy, accessible tools to help you arrange, plan, and organize your program. It offers a format with examples, detailed information, and suggestions to assist you in providing competent child care. *KIDEX for Infants* provides tools that assist communication between experienced staff members and new staff members. In addition, *KIDEX for Infants* provides forms and templates for keeping active files for each child and suggests a filing system for important information. Essentially, *KIDEX for Infants* will help you, the child care professional, fulfill your role in the daily care of the infants you are charged with.

HOW TO USE THIS BOOK

There are eight chapters, three perforated appendices, and a CD-ROM in the back of the book. Many chapters include examples of appropriate forms and/or templates necessary for rendering infant care. The Forms and Templates Appendix offers blank duplicates of the examples for you to photocopy, and the CD-ROM enables you to customize the forms according to your specific state standards and center requirements. The chapter examples (also indicated as figures) are there to guide you in completing your own forms when you are ready to use them.

KIDEX for Infants begins with suggestions for how to create a suitable environment equipped to render infant care and moves on to provide guidance and class management tools helpful for accomplishing physical care of the children. Where readers begin will depend on the degree of guidance they are seeking. For instance, someone in a brand new program would best start at the beginning and work through to the end. Someone in an already existing program searching to strengthen only certain aspects might choose to skip around the various chapters.

■ Chapter 1, "Typical Infant Behavior," profiles patterns and characteristics of infant behavior, and offers suggestions for establishing daily activities. Also covered are suitable expectations of babies during their first year of life.

■ Chapter 2, "Creating and Organizing the Infant Room Environment," provides guidance for creating environments that take into account infants' specific needs, best arranging the room to accommodate an infant group's natural tendencies, and accommodating their visiting family members.

■ Chapter 3, "Establishing an Excellent Path for Ongoing Communication," provides classroom management tools to maximize communication between the children's families and all personnel that are involved with your program on a daily basis. It also provides the tools for developing written plans beginning with detailed examples and instructions for assembling a KIDEX Class Book. A KIDEX Class Book is similar to an operating manual for your individual group. Use the examples and templates to write an organized plan for the infant group, including detailed daily schedules, individual profiles pertinent to babies' specific needs, lesson plans, and so forth.

■ Chapter 4, "Hygiene, Cleaning, and Disinfecting," will help you establish hygienic practices such as procedures for diapering, hand washing, and sanitation.

■ Chapter 5, "Health," provides guidance with regard to medications, measuring body temperatures, recording individual illnesses establishing practices to track illness trends, and other health tips.

■ Chapter 6, "Safety," addresses accident and incident reporting, establishing practices to track accident or incident trends, and how to conduct emergency evacuation drills. This chapter also provides tools for recording drills, first aid instructions, and other general safety practices.

■ Chapter 7, "Facilitating Baby and Baby's Family," provides suggestions that are conducive for rendering daily infant care and measures to include the family. The chapter suggests ways to assist both the child and the family from the moment the child is received in the center to daily departure. Some examples of forms include infant receiving sheets, the Introduce Us to Your Infant form, and individual child profiles for teachers to keep a written record of each individual infant's activities and progress.

■ Chapter 8, "Educational Articles for Families and Staff," provides short articles relevant to the care and understanding of infants. Use these articles to post on the Current Events Bulletin Board, to print in program newsletters, or as a basis for parenting and staff education classes. Store copies of these articles and other information you collect for the KIDEX Class Book for future reference.

FEATURES

■ Over 40 forms are available to assist child care professionals care for infants, including: nutrition schedules, observation sheets, diaper changing procedures, and daily medication sheets.

■ An icon appears throughout the book highlighting best practices.

■ Best Practices identified in the book are in alignment with CDA credential requirements.

BACK OF THE BOOK CD-ROM

■ Customizable forms are available on the back of the book CD-ROM.

Also available on CD:

■ state contact information to search for specific state rules and regulations

■ organizations listed with contact information for further research

■ additional resources for teachers and families

EACH STATE IS DIFFERENT

A directory listing of all state licensing agencies is available online on the National Resource Center for Child Care Health & Safety Web site at http://nrs.uchsc.edu. A reminder appears at the beginning of each chapter in the form of this icon:

To find your specific State's Licensing, Rules and Regulations go to:

http://nrc.uchsc.edu

It is extremely important to research the laws relevant to your own state licensing standards for compliance as well as to your specific child care center and/or facility.

Although you must follow state rules and regulations, most states require minimum standards. It is debatable whether state requirements reflect the highest level of care, also known as best practices. The term *best practices* comes from 981 standards identified by a panel of experts in the early 1990s. These standards were extracted from a compilation titled *Caring for Our Children* provided by three organizations: the American Academy of Pediatrics (AAP), the American Public Health Association (APHA), and the National Resource Center for Health and Safety. Best practices standards were identified as having the greatest impact on reducing frequent or severe disease, disability, and death (morbidity and mortality) in early education and child care settings. *KIDEX for Infants* incorporates these standards, and the following icon highlighting best practices appears in the margins to help you identify what is considered best practices.

KIDEX AND THE CDA CREDENTIAL

KIDEX for Infants incorporates essential information that aligns with many of the CDA competencies. There is a growing trend to raise the bar for child care practices in the United States. Many professional organizations manage accreditation systems for early care and teaching programs, such as the National Association of Educating Young Children (NAEYC), National Association of Child Care Professionals (NACCP), and National Association of Childcare (NAC). Accreditation is a voluntary process designed to improve the quality of child care programs by establishing benchmarks for quality. Caregivers who desire to be recognized for demonstrating competence in the early care and education field can pursue a Child Development Associate (CDA) credential. Candidates for the CDA credential are assessed based upon the CDA Competency Standards. The guidelines for the national CDA credential through the Council for Early Childhood Recognition can be found at http://www.cdacouncil.org.

ABOUT THE AUTHOR

Adrienne Boyd, R.N., B.S.N., has dedicated the majority of her professional life to the early care and education field. With over 22 years' experience in the field, Adrienne previously was executive director and co-owner of Somersett Heights Center for Child Care in Indianapolis. During that time she was active in the community, serving on the Governor's Task Force for Juvenile Justice, Indiana Task Force for Step Ahead Program, the advisory board for the local high school child care vocational school, and the Child Development Training Committee Workgroup on Early Care.

Adrienne served on the National Association of Child Care Professionals (NACCP) board, as a validator for the National Accreditation Commission for Early Child Care and Education Programs (NAC), and continues to serve the Editorial Advisory Board for *Early Childhood News,* a national publication for child care professionals.

In 1995, Adrienne and her husband, Bob, launched Child Development Services, Inc. Through this venue they published manuals, books, and child care training videos. She has received many Directors' Choice Awards for her work. She has contributed and published several articles for *Early Childhood News and Professional Connections,* the trade publication for the National Association of Child Care Professionals.

She is a mother of two grown sons, John and Alexander, and resides with her husband in Lebanon, Indiana.

ACKNOWLEDGMENTS

Throughout the process of writing this material, there were many individuals who supported, encouraged, and shared their expertise. I wish to extend my deepest gratitude to all of you.

To my husband, Bob, and two sons, John and Alexander, for accompanying me on my journey as owner and director of Somersett Heights Center for Child Care.

To Annette Wilson, who so patiently transcribed my writing. To Patricia Osborn, who provided editorial assistance during the revisions of this text. And to the Thomson Delmar Learning staff who caught my vision and helped to give birth to this project. To my sister Lois who so eloquently captures the imagination of children I have had the privilege of working with throughout my early care and education profession.

To my sister Nancy for her great love of children and for how it is a source of inspiration to me. And, finally, love and appreciation to my mother, Helen Struck, my very first teacher.

REVIEWERS

I would like to thank and acknowledge the following highly respected professionals in the child care field who provided invaluable suggestions, comments, and feedback on *KIDEX for Infants* to help make it the effective tool it is.

Vicki Folds, Ed.D.
Director of Curriculum Development
Children of America
Parkland, FL

Patricia Forkan, M.S.
Executive Director
TLC Learning Center
Blue Island, IL

Marsha Hutchinson, M.Ed.,
Executive Director
Polly Panda Preschool
Indianapolis, IN

Sally Harris
NACCP State Liaison and Validator
NAEYC Validator
Circle C Ranch Academy
Tampa, FL

Nan Howkins
Administrator, Child Care Consultant
The Children's Corner
Ridgefield, CT

Bonnie Malakie
Head Start Director Orleans
    Community Action Committee
Albion, NY

Lynnette McCarty, M.A.
President of NACCP
Executive Director
Serendipity Children's Center
Tumwater, WA

Wendy McEarchern, M.A.,
    Early Childhood Education
Executive Director
Gulf Regional Childcare
    Management Agency
Mobile, AL

Pamm Shaw, Executive Director
Berkeley-Albany YMCA Head Start
Berkeley, CA

To find your specific
State's Licensing, Rules
and Regulations go to:

http://nrc.uchsc.edu

Typical Infant Behavior

CHAPTER 1

JOURNEY THROUGH THE FIRST YEAR

Infants enter this world possessing their own distinct personalities. Although they have basically similar agendas such as eating, waking, sleeping, and eliminating, as well as patterns and bouts of cooing and crying, they will quickly establish their desire for routine based on their own unique internal drives. Until babies develop the physical ability to provide for themselves, they are completely dependent on others to meet their needs. It is important for the child care staff to create a pleasant experience.

Healthy babies normally follow a typical progression of development. Marhoefer and Vadnais (1988) remind us that "normal varies widely depending on the environment and the heritage of the child" (p. 281). Early care and education providers know that all infants develop at similar rates but in their own unique patterns. If it appears a baby is lagging behind other babies in certain areas, it could be due to many reasons, ranging from premature birth to a more reserved and cautious personality. Some babies are very cheerful and verbal in nature and seem to be delighted by a large variety of stimulating experiences. Other infants seem to be very focused and certain about how they prefer to be handled, and are quick to let you know their preferences. You will meet infants who are most content observing from afar, who are a bit shy and do not wish to be rushed with their activities of daily living. It is important to avoid a cookie-cutter approach for all infants and best to cue into their individual rhythms and styles as you create a schedule that works for them.

At birth a baby has a very large head in relation to its body. Special care must be taken to support a baby's head until the neck muscles become strong enough to support it. Because they do not have self-mobility yet, babies depend on you to provide them everything they need and desire.

Babies enjoy opportunities to look at objects—colorful or black and white—and like to explore all types of shapes and geometric forms. Baby gyms and mobiles are useful for displaying objects and appeal to babies while they rest on their backs. Babies respond to familiar faces and voices. They also pick up on voice tones as well. Your voice—through words, whispering, singing, and talking—contributes to their initial language development. It is important to note that when they are very young they can reach a point of overstimulation, especially in a busy infant room. Care must be taken to avoid overstimulation and sensory overload. If a baby is suddenly disinterested or becomes fussy, he or she might be indicating a need for cuddling and quiet time.

By their third month, babies express joy through laughter and smiles. Once they can hold their head without assistance they can begin playing and exploring on a new level. They often will have some favorite toys they like to reach for. They respond to games such as peek-a-boo, love to explore books with help, and are fascinated by noisy toys, especially the ones they can shake.

Sometime around the fourth or fifth month, a baby will begin to turn over. Make it a habit to keep a hand on a baby, from day one, especially when the baby is in a vulnerable spot such as on a diaper changing table. Their ability to turn over independently often happens quickly with little or no warning. To avoid strangulation accidents, remove cords on their clothing and avoid attaching objects such as pacifiers to their clothing. Once they begin to sit up, remove crib toys such as mobiles from their beds for the same reason.

At six months their world continues to change rapidly. Their bodies are developing and they are now able to use their arms and legs more purposefully. Most babies are able to sit unassisted, and the more adventurous ones could begin exploring by scooting. Once they have established a strong sitting posture they are able to sit in a high chair and begin drinking from a cup for some of their liquids and feeding themselves some finger foods. Be careful to choose foods a baby can manage with few or no teeth. By now most babies will have developed a huge appetite for new experiences. They play and learn by touching, holding, and mouthing objects. Babies experience true delight banging objects in order to create lots of noise. They will continue using both their right and left hand without preference. Hand preference will not be determined for some time. Their verbal skills continue to develop and they spend a great deal of time babbling and talking in their own language. Babies will experience moments of frustration when their desire to communicate is thwarted by their limited speech abilities. Teaching and using sign language symbols with babies is a very successful growing trend in this country. Recommended resources for this practice are located in Chapter 7, "Facilitating Baby and Baby's Family."

STRANGER ANXIETY

It is not uncommon around six or eight months for a baby to develop "stranger fear." Wong (1999) relates "the infant's ability to distinguish between familiar and nonfamiliar people. Behaviors such as clinging to the parent, crying, and turning away from the stranger are common" (p. 572). Babies will need time to adjust to unfamiliar people. Holding them close and providing them time to warm up to a new person often helps.

By nine to twelve months babies try to pull up with the assistance of furniture or your leg! They move around the room crawling, scooting, and creeping. It is natural for them to explore with all parts of their body. They are very pleased with their progressing skills and often can be observed moving about with a toy in their hand. Now, more than ever, their environment will need to be "baby proofed" since they are incapable of distinguishing between what is safe and what is dangerous. And watch out: your earrings, necklaces, or other reachable items such as electrical cords attached to crock pots and coffee pots are easy to grab. Because scalding accidents are common among small babies, best practices discourage drinking hot beverages in their environment. By now a baby understands simple directives and is saying words such as mama and dada and commonly will add more words as they approach their first birthday. A baby will especially enjoy activities like putting items in containers and dumping them, dropping objects and watching you pick them up, scribbling on paper with a large crayon, and attempting to feed himself or herself with a spoon—although babies will not have mastered the use of a spoon and will use their other hand to complete the mission.

SEPARATION ANXIETY

Herr (1994) notes that "somewhere between nine and twelve months some children have difficulty separating from their main caregiver, usually mom. You might find that children experiencing this anxiety will cry each day when their parents leave them at the center" (p. 398). This can be a gut-wrenching feeling for the parent. Reassure the parents that this is a normal stage and it will usually pass within a few weeks once the little one becomes more familiar with the center. Encourage parents with older infants to visit the center with their child several times prior to the first day to help with their child's transition. Spending time in the infant room prior to beginning care will also help new parents feel more comfortable. Most infants by now have adopted an item they enjoy cuddling with, such as a favorite doll, stuffed animal, or blanket. Encourage the use of their favorite comfort item, especially during the transition. Their comfort item demonstrates their growth in the area of self-comfort.

Sometimes new parents are overwhelmed with the care of their newest family member and can't imagine how a teacher could possibly manage the care of several infants at once. Their fears are quickly alleviated once they realize the teachers in an early care and teaching environment dedicate their time and energy solely to the children they care for, and are not distracted by phone calls, cleaning house, or washing laundry. Understanding the needs of new parents in their fragile state is further explored in Chapter 7, "Facilitating Baby and Baby's Family."

For the most part, the first year in an infant's life will be greatly supported by adults who devote their time to providing measures of enrichment, safety, and security through voice modulation, patience, gentle touch, and joyful, happy interactions and who quickly respond to the baby's requests. As babies move toward their toddler years, they will need continual recognition and encouragement as they learn and practice new skills. A strong understanding of normal growth and development is essential for early care and learning professionals. Staying abreast of new discoveries through ongoing research is vital for continual professional development. Babies cared for by teachers who are "lifetime learners" will always benefit from the new information learned and employed in the environments created for them.

REFERENCES

Herr, J. (1994). *Working with young children.* Tinely Park, IL: The Goodheart-Willcox Company.

Marhoefer, P. E., & Vadnais, L. A. (1988). *Caring for the developing child.* Clifton Park, NY: Thomson Delmar Learning.

Wong, D. (1999). *Whaley & Wong's nursing care of infants and children* (6th ed.). St. Louis, MO: Mosby.

RECOMMENDED RESOURCES

Ellison, S., & Ferdinandi, S. (1996). *365 days of baby love.* Naperville, IL: Sourcebook.

Fisher, J. J. (1988). *From baby to toddler.* New York: The Berkley Publishing Group.

Fraiberg, S. H. (1987). *The magic years.* New York: Fireside. (Original work published 1959)

Reisser, P. C. (1997). *Baby & child care.* Carol Stream, IL: Tyndale House.

HELPFUL WEB SITES

Talaris Research Institute, *Advancing knowledge of early brain development.* Retrieved from http://www.talaris.org.

CHAPTER 2

Creating and Organizing the Infant Room Environment

To find your specific State's Licensing, Rules and Regulations go to:

http://nrc.uchsc.edu

The quality of a child's environment can have a significant impact on his or her emotional well-being. Healthy children require a safe physical environment in which to eat, sleep, and play in order to accommodate their growth and developmental needs. A well thought out, properly equipped, clean, organized, and well-maintained environment will support their growing needs (see Figures 2–1 and 2–2 for an example of infant room layout and arrangements).

SQUARE FOOTAGE CONSIDERATIONS

You must consider many factors when designing a successful infant room. There is always a fine balance between meeting the local government mandates and considering the cost of your finished space. Many states and governing bodies require minimum standards to issue an operating license. Often the minimum standards are based on old regulations and do not take into consideration the ever increasing influx of new baby equipment available

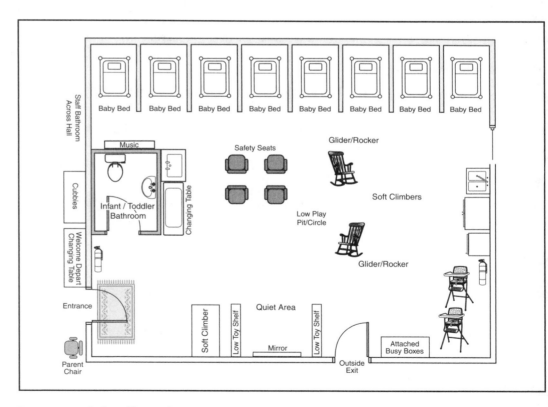

FIGURE 2–1 Infant Room Layout

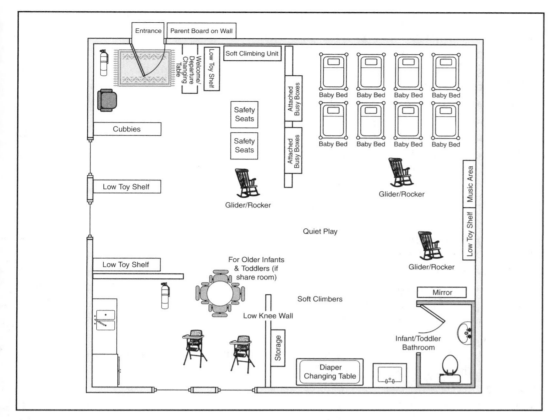

FIGURE 2–2 Infant Room Layout

today. Climbing lofts, saucers, soft climbers, and strollers designed for multiple babies are just a few items you may need room for. On the other hand, creating and equipping an infant room requires careful planning if you are to remain financially solvent. Square footage costs vary among regions and will determine the most financially feasible size for a facility. Allow for around 50–100 square feet indoors per infant as a starting consideration.

SLEEPING AND RESTING AREA

If space is limited, creativity and careful planning will be needed to accommodate sleeping and resting areas. Place the cribs in one area of the room to create a quiet atmosphere if possible. Plan at least 3 feet between cribs to reduce the possibility of germ cross-contamination when babies occupy them. If space is restricted, then consider having dedicated storage beneath each crib for each infant's personal belongings, especially if your program uses cribs for changing diapers.

Cribs tend to use a great deal of space. Programs in cramped spaces might consider using Plexiglas crib cubbies. Building Plexiglas walls between cribs is one way to reduce the 3-foot requirement between cribs yet still avoid cross-contamination. The Plexiglas crib cubbies free up space for other uses. The Plexiglas walls separating each crib allow an open feeling, and resting babies can see into the other cribs. Place sturdy casters on the cribs to pull them in and out of the bed cubbies (see Figure 2–1). The casters will also make the beds usable in the event of an emergency evacuation. Cribs with Plexiglas viewing footboards are recommended. Plexiglas footboards increase the ability of teachers to view an infant occupying a crib from a sitting position when they are busy feeding or rocking another infant. This particular crib is readily available.

Most infants, early on, establish specific routines and preferences that assist with their relaxation and napping. Some infants enjoy rocking and cuddling prior to their napping periods. Others might sing and babble or enjoy playing quietly until they drift off. A gliding chair provides a rocking motion without the hazard of pinching crawling babies' fingers. Glider rocking chairs are available in large infant superstores and can be found at Early Childhood Manufacturers' Direct at http://www.ECMDStore.com or 1-800-896-9951. To accommodate babies' individual routines, place several glider chairs near the napping area and create a quiet play area for infants not quite ready to sleep. This will also provide an area for those babies who are slow to awaken and rejoin the group. Stock this area with cloth books, perhaps a wall mirror, and a selection of quiet toys.

Because some child care providers use playpens as a quiet area to establish boundaries for an infant, it is important to address the most current trend of thinking among "best practice" professionals. Most states' licensing regulators prohibit using playpens or baby cribs for any other reason than sleeping or diaper changing. Child care providers in early care and education environments plan programs integrated with the best child development practices. They strongly discourage the use of equipment that restricts a child's physical movements such as swings, walkers, playpens, and cribs used for play spaces. Restricting babies' ability to move slows down their potential development and their ability to explore their bodies' without restraint. If they are subjected to long periods in restrictive equipment, their stimulating experiences are reduced, deterring their healthy growth and development.

If you want to create a barrier between the quiet resting area and the active areas, consider several choices. Some programs opt for a wall with viewing windows to separate the groups. Many state regulators and licensing agencies consider this option a separate room and will require it to be fully staffed any time an infant occupies a crib. Keep in mind that infants commonly adapt to the usual infant room noises. Once they are accustomed to the routines in their group, they no longer seem disturbed by common activities and are quite able to sleep in a room occupied by other verbal infants. Another option to consider is a knee wall allowing for a division between areas without creating two rooms. The knee wall is helpful to discourage crawling infants from "visiting" the resting infants. Check your local regulators: knee walls are considered in some states to constitute a separate room and are prohibited. For crib recommendations, as well as safe handling of infant linens and crib toys such as mobiles, see Chapters 4 through 6 on hygiene, health, and safety.

BATHROOMS AND DIAPERING AREA

Why install a bathroom in an infant room? Some state licensing regulators require that a bathroom be installed in a room to accommodate the care of infants and that staff be prohibited from using this bathroom for their own use. An additional bathroom will need to be provided for staff. Place it either in the infant room if plenty of space is available, or in close proximity to the room, to promote teacher comfort and reduce extended time away. Arrangements for bathroom breaks will need to be planned to maintain steady child/staff ratios throughout the day. Nurseries that maintain recommended children/staff ratios experience fewer accidents.

Although infants are not expected to toilet train at such a young age, flushing toilets are useful for discarding soiled soap and water created by daily cleansing of soiled diapers and soiled clothing containers. Most early care and education environments opt to use disposable diapers, training pants, bibs, or wipes in place of cloth in order to promote the highest level of sanitary practice. However, sometimes children are allergic to the materials found in disposable diapers and require the use of cloth diapers. If cloth diapers are used for children with medical conditions such as allergies, special handling will be necessary to ensure hygiene and safety for the handlers. This subject is explored in greater detail in Chapter 4, "Hygiene, Cleaning, and Disinfecting."

In some parts of the country it is not uncommon to mix infants and toddlers in one group. The majority of toddlers are well into age two before they toilet train. Occasionally some precocious toddlers have been known to toilet train well ahead of the usual schedule. A bathroom will serve their needs if the occasion arises.

Sometimes current demand for a certain age group shifts within a center's enrollment, requiring that a room be changed to accommodate another age group. In that case a center might change an infant room into a toddler or preschool room as the demand for a specific age group fluctuates. Plumbing each room for that possibility will save time and money if a change is demanded in the future.

Special child-size flushing toilets are available through most plumbing sources. Provide room for portable potty chairs if your licensing agency allows for them. Instruct the plumber to install the sink(s) at a child's height. Make provisions to equip all sources of hot water with antiscald devices to avoid potential hot water burns and scalding.

Set up the diaper changing area with the following equipment. Choose a smooth, nonabsorbent easy-to-clean surface. Do not plan on using areas that come in close contact with children during play, such as couches, the floor in play areas, and so on. Many suitable commercial diaper changing units are on the market. Check the list of recommended resources for sources. Disposable items and supplies used for the actual diapering process are detailed in the discussion of diaper changing procedures in Chapter 4, "Hygiene, Cleaning, and Disinfecting." Provide a continuous source of hot, running water from a sink positioned at an adult height. Install soap, towel dispensers, and a diaper changing table that is nonabsorbent and able to withstand continual disinfecting applications. Attach shelves with dividers near the changing area to store each infant's diaper supplies so they do not touch another's personal supply. Plastic bags are required in some states for soiled diapers, and they are necessary for enclosing soiled clothing. Install a container to store plastic bags in so they are safely out of the reach of the little ones. Best practices encourage placing soiled disposable diapers, wipes, tissues, and gloves in a plastic-lined, hands-free, covered can. If a child's medical condition requires cloth diapers, you will need a separate, covered, plastic-lined, hands-free container to store them until pickup. Although the rules vary from state to state, best practices advise the use of disposable gloves as part of the hygienic measures during diapering procedures. Hang a bulletin board near the changing table to post hand washing and disinfecting procedures, diaper changing checklists, special notes, and "sharing time" discussion items.

KITCHEN AND EATING AREA

Food safety is an important component to consider when creating an environment for infant food preparation and storage. Young babies are especially susceptible to bacteria. The USDA (2000) reports "children under 5 are susceptible to food-borne illnesses because their immune systems are not fully developed" (p. 9). Creating a space to accommodate food preparation and feeding the infants is extremely important.

Once again it is important to check your local regulating bodies for guidance specific to your area. Some states require the parents to prepare the bottles at home and label them with the child's name, the contents of the bottle, and the time and date it was prepared. Other states strictly prohibit this practice and require that child care staff prepare bottles at the center. Furthermore, there are specific laws that only allow for ready-to-feed formulas and do not allow the use of concentrated or powdered formulas that require mixing unless the infant's doctor indicates in writing that the baby is allergic to the first kind. The logic behind prohibiting formulas that call for mixing is that formulas can be mixed too rich or too thin, causing improper nutrition for the infant.

In the kitchen, provide a full-size refrigerator/freezer to accommodate the formulas, prepared bottles, foods, and medications. Place a kitchen thermometer in the refrigerator to monitor temperatures. The refrigerator should be cooled to 41°F or less and the freezer to 0°F or less. Your local health and fire regulators govern the use of an oven or stove. Since sterilizing bottles and their pieces involves boiling water, it should take place in a state board of health–approved kitchen environment away from the children. If the bottles are prepared in a separate area it will require additional personnel so proper child/staff ratios can be maintained. Preparing bottles is a time-consuming task and requires strict attention to details. Preparing bottles on site will require plenty of counterspace. A couple of roomy cabinets are quite useful for storage: baby cereals, formula, and jarred foods in one, and clean bottles, nipples, collars, and disposable bottle liners in another.

You will need to consider several types of eating arrangements based on the span of ages you are caring for. For infants 1–12 months old, provide several safety seats, with straps, constructed at an angle allowing a slight recline for infants who are unable to sit unsupported; and several high chairs equipped with straps and sanitizable surfaces. For specific feeding instructions, refer to Chapter 7, "Facilitating Baby and Baby's Family." In some states the use of high chairs is prohibited. Check the regulation mandates for your area.

ACTIVE AREA

Babies naturally learn a great deal using their bodies. They learn about themselves and the world they live in by exploring their own bodies and how they relate to their environment. When they begin to move about they will not yet have the ability to understand boundaries. Create a safe place for infants to facilitate learning and exploring. For instance, create areas separated by low, open, sturdy toy shelves to separate quiet activities such as reading time and active play spaces that facilitate toy play so either can be enjoyed without interruption by others. Soft toy boxes with low sides, easy for babies to crawl in and out of, are readily available on the market. They are manufactured in a variety of shapes. You can place a few toys in one and provide easy access for a baby. These soft toy shapes are ideal for creating a space for an infant to enjoy solitary play in a protected spot while others play around him or her. Complex soft climbing units are also a wonderful addition to any infant room. They are designed at a safe height, conducive for infants to crawl on, around, and through. They are available with tunnels, small slides easy for baby to negotiate, and one or two steps to practice climbing up and down. See the end of this chapter for suggested resources.

Also consider using unbreakable safety mirrors to enhance babies' exploration. You can provide a steady supply of interesting pictures in acrylic frames to ponder and talk about, mounted to the wall at babies' eye level. Attach busy boxes at heights for babies to play with both seated and standing. A little pull-up bar or ballet bar assists the older infant who is just beginning to stand and walk. If toddlers share space with the infants, add a low table and chairs designed with sides for art exploration and table play.

OUTDOOR PLAY SPACES

Give infants opportunities to play outdoors. It is important to provide a space for infants to play separate from older children. Many state licensing agencies require separated playgrounds for infants and toddlers. Infants' play habits are completely different and they need more supervision. Provide the infants play equipment and materials suitable for their level of development.

A great deal of planning is necessary to design and construct a modern playground that is equipped with safe materials and play equipment that is also accessible to children with special needs. Playgrounds today need to offer children opportunities to use their bodies and imagination. The play equipment and surfaces need to conform to recommendations from the American with Disabilities Act (ADA). For guidance to build, equip, and inspect a playground that meets all suggested standards of accessibility and safety requirements, refer to the recommended resources at the end of this chapter.

MUSIC AND LIGHTING

Sunlight, bright lighting, and peaceful music and sounds provide a sense of well-being and can encourage pleasant and cheerful feelings among those who occupy the space. It is a well-documented fact that children require low-stress environments to thrive. Provide several sources of music and lighting to enhance the infant room and promote a peaceful, homelike atmosphere. Soft lighting is soothing for resting and napping infants. Wire the rooms to create soft lighting in the resting and quiet areas. Table lamps are another alternative if wiring a more sophisticated lighting pattern is not feasible. Skylights also provide a gentle, natural lighting source. Check with your local licensing agents to determine the amount of lighting mandated during infants' waking and sleeping times, since requirements vary from state to state.

Current research tells us that reading and singing to children are simple and effective ways to promote brain development. One *ABC Primetime* producer (Harrington 1994) reported that music serves many functions in the infant room. Scientific research has linked the use of music with increasing brain development. A PET scan (positron-emission tomography) scans and measures brain activities, producing actual pictures that demonstrate that once stimulation is applied repetitively, in a positive fashion, the brain sprouts connections and grows new pathways. Activities such as singing, playing, and listening to music support positive change in the brain and increase intelligence. Studies have demonstrated that Mozart, Classical, and Baroque music, strengthens the pathways in the brain for future math development! Babies are absolutely delighted by many different musical experiences. Feel free to experiment with a wide variety of music from classical lullabies to the exciting sounds of marching and parade music. A vast amount of literature described how the brain develops in the early years and suggests measures to facilitate growth. The National Child Care Information Centers (NCCIC) is a national clearinghouse and technical assistance center. Its mission is to link parents, providers, policy makers, researchers, and the public to early care and education information (http://www.nccic.org).

AGE-APPROPRIATE TOYS FOR INFANTS

Throughout the first year an infant's need for toys will consistently change with development. A newborn is basically passive and enjoys toys that he or she can see or listen to. Later, as a baby's skills and abilities change, he or she will prefer active, hands-on toys. Toys best suited for infants are colorful or have contrasting colors, are lightweight, and offer a variety of textures. Popular are small and large soft blocks; toys that can be squeezed, pushed, rolled, or rattled; toys that provide opportunities to dump and fill; toys that can be taken apart and fit back together; toys that create reaction from action (cause and effect); and musical instruments suitable for an infant. Suggested lists of specific toys are outlined in Figures 2–3, 2–4, 2–5, and 2–6.

Suggested Toys for Infants 1–3 Months	
■ rattle	■ toy that emits sounds when touched
■ 2 or 3 soft scarflike materials	■ mirrored toy
■ 1 or 2 books of simple pictures	■ large toys baby can hold
■ music box or toy	■ 2 or 3 soft fabrics
■ puppet or stuffed animal	■ 1 or 2 rubber squeeze toys
■ mobile or colored rings	■ animal pictures
■ a straw (teacher only)	■ brightly colored cubes or blocks
■ access to a mirror at baby's height	■ transparent rattle
■ 2 or 3 color cards	■ string of sturdy bells
■ taped music	

FIGURE 2–3 Suggested Toys 1–3 Months

Careful consideration is required to select safe toys that match infants' developmental abilities and appropriate skills. Infants often place inappropriate objects into their mouths. Toys that are smaller than a tennis ball are not recommended. The toys must be sturdy and free of detachable pieces that might be swallowed. Avoid stuffed animals or dolls with detachable eyes, such as button eyes. Stuffed animals should be individually labeled and used by one infant only. Choose toys that are washable.

Brain development research has provided sound evidence that reading to children for as little as 15–20 minutes per day from an early age contributes to a myriad of positive brain developments. Early care and education professionals are well aware that reading helps develop children's attention span, builds vocabularies, enhances self-esteem, increases the ability to visualize and imagine, and provides many opportunities to understand words and spoken language. Based on this evidence, an enriched environment for infants is filled with pictures, both black and white and in color, using a variety of geometric forms and bright objects, and books that contain simple stories, rhymes, and finger plays. Washable cloth and plastic books are recommended for an infant. Avoid paper books at this age unless babies are closely supervised. They are fascinated with the sound of paper ripping and do not possess enough information to understand this is not an acceptable practice. Torn paper invites chewing and the pieces can cause babies to choke. The following teacher-recommended books are good choices:

Some Suggested Books to Read to Infants

Green Eggs and Ham by Dr. Seuss

The Very Hungry Caterpillar by Eric Carle

Bread and Jam for Frances by Russell Hoban

Scrambled Egg Supper! by Dr. Seuss

The Carrot Seed by Ruth Krauss

Alphabet Soup by Kate Banks

Jamberry by Bruce Degan

Little Whistle's Dinner Party by Cynthia Rylant

Sweet Dream Pie by Audrey Woods

Today Is Monday by Eric Carle

Suggested Toys for Infants 4–6 Months

- baby's personal large soft stuffed animals
- washable activity mat or a large patterned cloth
- 1 or 2 washable squeak toys
- book of simple nursery rhymes
- simple household items: spoon, alarm clock, towel, etc.
- 4 or 5 pictures of happy faces
- large beach ball
- pictures of kittens, dogs, house pets
- 2 or 3 rings 2"–5" wide
- blowing bubbles (teacher only)
- farm animal pictures or Fisher Price Farm Animal Sounds toy
- container of small washable brightly colored pictures
- baby jumper seat or bouncer
- 2 or 3 different size balls
- toys that create noise (plastic spatula & pans)
- pictures of different flowers

- pictures of animals: zoo, farm animals
- taped music
- tape of bird sounds
- 2 or 3 simple, washable books to share w/baby at story time
- 2 or 3 rattles
- dishpan full of washable, colorful blocks
- small hand-size toys
- laminated pictures
- several metal spoons
- cup (small enough for baby to hold)
- plastic pop beads
- transparent toys
- book of nursery rhymes
- several small washable books
- large bead necklace (securely fastened)
- tape of parade music
- nesting cups

FIGURE 2–4 Suggested Toys 4–6 Months

Toys used in an infant environment require careful selection to promote safe exploration and play. Avoid toys with long cords or strings in order to avoid strangulation. Steer clear of toys with small pieces to avoid choking incidents. Supply toys babies can hold and manipulate, choosing items in a variety of colors, sizes, and shapes. Make available sturdy rattles or make your own shakers. Remember to construct them with nontoxic materials and glue the lids shut to avoid access to contents inside. Choose sturdy toys that can withstand heavy usage and many rounds of washing and disinfecting. Check toys and equipment frequently for wear and tear. Sharp edges and broken pieces are a potential danger; remove them immediately.

CHOOSING TOYS WITH CULTURAL DIVERSITY IN MIND

Responsible early care and teaching programs strive to address diversity in the classroom. Special thought and planning are required to create a diverse environment that is considerate of different genders and racial and ethnic differences encountered within our population. In order to integrate appropriate practices, choose toys that include all the backgrounds and cultures represented in our population and in your classroom. Make an effort to choose dolls with different colored skins. Display pictures that represent all nationalities. Seek help from the parents to explore other areas such as food, words children are familiar with, music they hear in their own family environment, or special holidays they celebrate. Parents will appreciate your effort to include them in the process of integrating practices that recognize the various cultures their children represent.

Suggested Toys for Infants 7–9 Months

- 2 or 3 musical tapes with different even beats
- nursery rhymes book
- 3 or 4 books that feature babies doing activities
- animal book . . . *especially animals doing things babies do!!*
- wind-up alarm clock
- 3 empty plastic containers with lids (Poke holes in lids. Put scent on cotton balls individually. Use cinnamon, vanilla, & peppermint. Store each pile of scented cotton balls in a different container. Secure lids tightly for baby to smell.)
- soft fuzzy sock to fit over baby bottle
- soap bubbles
- several different textured rug squares
- several different feathers (teacher only)
- tape of familiar sounds
- spoon, small sturdy pan, & small cloth
- sturdy cards with designs laminated so they are washable
- plain paper, tape, fat crayons
- old or used computer paper for crumbling

- 2" cubes or plastic blocks
- 1 or 2 Raggedy Annes or Andys or washable soft doll
- toy telephone
- 2 or 3 different size balls
- 7–10 nature pictures of leaves, bugs, birds, flowers, etc.
- baby doll
- metal spoons
- shoe
- 1 or 2 different washable puppets
- large blocks *(soft type preferable)*
- 3 or 4 different hats
- several pans with lids, large plastic spoons
- 7–10 pictures (laminated) of people working & playing
- old easy-to-open purse (fill with comb, keys, brush, or other washable items)
- nesting blocks or several plastic bowls that fit inside each other, or measuring cups

FIGURE 2–5 Suggested Toys 7–9 Months

Carol J. Fuhler, author of *Teaching Reading with Multicultural Books Kids Love,* is an excellent resource. She encourages many approaches for a teacher to integrate multicultural teachings relevant in today's culturally diverse society. "[For children] to make a strong connection with a book, to elicit that all-important affective response, every child should see his or her face reflected in some of the illustrations. His or her culture should be explored realistically within well-crafted stories" (p. *x*). A teacher who continually makes a deliberate effort to integrate and explore differences and likenesses among all people will provide an environment that communicates acceptance for all children he or she cares for.

NUTRITION SCHEDULE BULLETIN BOARD

Establishing routines and practices that assure nutrition is delivered in a timely and accurate fashion is vital for proper nutrition and comfort. Specific information needed to provide individualized care for each infant must be accessible at all times. The information must be described in a manner that is easy to understand and available for use at a moment's notice. A hungry infant deserves immediate attention and will benefit from having an organized plan in place. Although every infant room has a core group of teachers who are usually very familiar with each infant's daily routines, several part-time and substitute teachers will be required to help accommodate the long shift hours, family

Suggested Toys for Infants 10–12 Months	
■ blocks & container	■ pictures in books or laminated pictures of food (such as cookie, banana, apple, cracker, toast)
■ 5 or 6 canning jar lids & washable string	■ pictures in books or laminated pictures of clothes (such as shoes, hat, socks, pants, coat)
■ several books with pages that baby can turn with ease	■ soap bubbles, toy car
■ pan & plastic spoon to make a drum	■ medium-size plastic baby keys, stacking rings
■ toy piano or music toy that reacts with ease when touched	■ large nesting cups
■ pictures of animals (laminated or in a vinyl book)	■ set of large duplo blocks, simple sorter
■ small toys for baby to practice grasping	■ dress-up clothes (large t-shirt, big shoes, hats)
■ milk jug with handle filled with ½ cup of dry beans (glue lid on permanently)	■ push toys such as corn popper, lawn mower
■ clean whisk broom	■ washable pictures of modes of transportation (boats, trains, cars, etc.)
■ variety of sturdy bells, can of tennis balls with lid, coasters, or canning rings	■ pull toy that doesn't topple easily
■ 3 or 4 choices of paired items for baby to match (2 socks, 2 alike toys, etc.)	■ 4 or 5 books that tell simple stories
■ milk jug with washable clothespins (no springs)	■ 6 or 7 matching pairs in container
■ plastic container & lid easy for baby to remove	■ several balls, different sizes, textures, & weights
■ riding/pushing car/horse (no pedals)	■ push cart with play dishes
■ books with everyday items (Richard Scarry, *Things That Go*)	■ simple slide that easily stores when not in use
	■ firm pillow or soft climber for climbing
■ soft music tapes, lively fun music tapes	■ musical instruments that are washable & not too small to avoid being swallowed
	■ vocabulary book (durable & washable)

FIGURE 2–6 Suggested Toys 10–12 Months

work schedules, breaks, lunches, staff vacations, and so forth. At each staff transition, a caregiver usually requires a few moments to orient to an infant room environment and assimilate the babies' current needs. A current nutrition schedule bulletin board provides a transition bridge, allowing the substitute teachers to respond to each baby quickly and in an accurate manner.

Bear in mind some states require parents to prepare bottles and bring them properly labeled for use by the center each day. Other state licensing agencies require the center personnel to handle bottle preparation exclusively. Check your local agency for guidance. Dedicate a dry erase or chalk board in the infant room to the nutrition schedule. Hang the board in a location that is easy to see. The primary purpose of the nutrition schedule bulletin board is to provide a place to clearly outline each infant's nutrition schedule and requirements, and identify specific supplies needed to perform each task. (Note: This board is not used to record daily individual feedings. Record that information on infant daily observation sheets (see Figure 3–12 in Chapter 3). Figure 2–7 provides an example of a nutrition schedule bulletin board. Use a permanent marker to create permanent categories based on the hours the infant room operates. Tailor the categories based on your licensing requirements. Suggested categories are: all infants' names, breakfast, AM snack/beverage, lunch, and PM snack/beverage, a dinner slot, snack or evening feeding, and

Nutrition Schedule Bulletin Board

Baby's Name	Breakfast/ Beverage	Snack/ Beverage	Lunch/ Beverage	Snack/ Beverage	Dinner/ Beverage	Snacks	Bottle Type	Nipple Type	Pacifier
Jackson (Enter Last Name)	3T Rice cereal 3T Fruit 6–8 oz Similac	1 c. Vit C Fruit Juice Toast	6–8 oz Similac 2T Meat 2–6T Potatoes 5–9T Veg 4–6T Fruit	6–8 oz Similac	HOME	HOME	EVENFLO	EVENFLO	NUK
Hailey (Enter Last Name)	6–8 oz Breast Milk	4–6 oz Sterile Water	4–6 oz Breast Milk	4–6 oz Sterile Water	4–6 oz Breast Milk	4–6 oz Breast Milk	MUNCHKIN Newborn	MUNCHKIN Newborn	Baby Buddy
Ian (Enter Last Name)	4–6 T Cereal 4–6 T Fruit 5–8 oz Enfalac	Juice	Whole Jar Meat 2 T Veg Jar	HOME	HOME	HOME	GERBER	DR. BROWN'S	NONE
Emily (Enter Last Name)	2–3 T Oatmeal Cereal	6 oz Enfamil	2–3 T Fruit 2–3 T Veg	2 Crackers 6 oz Enfamil	HOME	HOME	PLAYTEX	PLAYTEX	Baby Buddy
Sydney (Enter Last Name)	Scrambled Egg Toast	1 c. Organic Whole Milk or Juice	2T Meat 2–6 T Rice 5–9 T Veg 4–6 T Fruit	1 c. Organic Whole Milk Toast 2 Crackers	HOME	HOME	EVENFLO	EVENFLO	Tommy Tippee
Emma (Enter Last Name)	2–3 T Cereal 2–3 T Fruit 5–7 oz Breast Milk	4 oz Juice	5–7 oz Breast Milk 2 Crackers	5–7 oz Breast Milk	5–7 oz Breast Milk 2–3T Oatmeal Cereal	HOME	PLAYTEX	PLAYTEX	NONE
Joseph (Enter Last Name)	5–8 oz Breast Milk	5–8 oz Breast Milk	5–8 oz Breast Milk Toast 2 Crackers	5–8 oz Breast Milk	2 T Rice Cereal	5–8 oz Breast Milk	EVENFLO	GERBER	NONE
Kaylie (Enter Last Name)	5–8 oz Breast Milk	5–8 oz Breast Milk	5–8 oz Breast Milk Toast 2 Crackers	5–8 oz Breast Milk	2 T Rice Cereal	5–8 oz Breast Milk	DR. BROWN'S	DR. BROWN'S	NUK

FIGURE 2–7 Nutrition Schedule Board

2:00 AM time slot if you operate at night. Include a box for the type of bottle, nipple, and pacifier. There are many brands available and a baby will not enjoy one he or she is not accustomed to. This board is extremely handy for a quick reference throughout the day. It is especially helpful for substitute teachers and aides. It promotes efficiency in the busy infant room and reduces the chance of error. If wall space is limited then it is advisable for the teachers to complete the empty template (see the Forms and Templates Appendix). Place completed template in the KIDEX Class Book. Train all substitutes to refer to the centrally located KIDEX Class Book in each room for this information.

CUBBIES/STORAGE OF PERSONAL BELONGINGS

In an effort to keep track of the many personal effects provided to render care and avoid potential cross-contamination, storage of personal belongings will need careful consideration. Personal belongings such as coats, hats, and extra baby clothing are best kept in separate cubbies. If possible, create a space just outside of the infant room door or near the entrance. Provide a sturdy wide shelving unit that houses baskets, waist high for parents/guardians to remove babies' outdoor clothing at arrival and departure time. Provide an individual basket for each infant. Place an adult chair for parents to sit for added convenience. Placing the cubbies outside the room or in the vestibule will discourage the crawling infants from exploring each basket uninvited during the day! An alternative is commercial cubby or locker units that are widely marketed in school catalogues such as Discount School Supply (http://www.DiscountSchoolSupply.com or 1-800-627-2829) or KAPLAN Early Learning Company (http://www.kaplanco.com or 1-800-334-2014).

ROOM APPEARANCE AND CLEANING CHECKLIST

It doesn't take long for a busy infant room to begin to clutter. Without a consistent effort to maintain order, the room appearance and safety will become compromised. A room strewn with soiled bibs, empty bottles, and unkempt toys is not only unsightly but has the potential to be unhealthy.

A routine for handling soiled toys, bottles, bottle accessories, and clothing is covered in detail in Chapter 4, "Hygiene, Cleaning, and Disinfecting." To keep up your center's appearance and maintain a safe environment, always make an effort to reduce clutter in your environment and maintain cleanliness. Imagine how you prepare your home for a party before guests arrive. You usually survey the house and stow all miscellaneous clutter in its proper place. The floors are vacuumed, dust is removed, fingerprints are washed away, and disinfection procedures are employed, leaving the room sparkling and clean. Fresh flowers are always a nice touch. You are motivated to create a pleasant environment for the guests you are about to receive. The pleasant care environment you create not only promotes your own comfort; it reflects your best intentions for the babies. Think about the environment you create for them. Imagine daily that it is your grand opening day. Look around the room and see where a pile of clutter has begun to form. Are toys scattered about the room creating a potential for tripping or falling? Are used baby bottles or soiled blankets strewn around? Your room organization is an ongoing routine requiring clearing off, cleaning up, and putting away. Post a cleaning schedule (Figure 2–8) for all to follow. Every extra effort you make does make a big difference. Remember, your environment is a reflection of you!

Cleaning Schedule

For the Week of: _1/15–1/2_

Classroom: _B_

Daily Cleaning Projects	Mon	Tue	Wed	Thr	Fri	Once-A-Week Projects	Initial	Date
1. Mop floors	X	X	X	X	X	Scrub brush & mop (corners)	MS	1/8
2. Clean all sinks (use cleanser)	X	X	X	X	X	Wipe down all bathroom walls	MS	1/20
3. Wipe down walls (around sinks)	X	X	X	X	X	Scrub step stools	MS	1/6
4. Clean & disinfect toilets (with brush in & out)	X	X	X	X	X	Use toothbrush on fountain (mouth piece)	N/A	N/A
5. Clean water fountains/wipe with disinfectant	X	X	X	X	X	Clean windows	MS	1/20
6. Clean inside of windows and seals	X	X	X	X	X	Wipe off door handles	MS	1/20
7. Clean inside & outside glass on doors	X	X	X	X	X	Organize shelves	MS	1/5
8. Clean & disinfect changing table & under the pad	X	X	X	X	X	Move furniture and sweep	MS	1/6
9. Run vacuum (carpet & rugs)	X	X	X	X	X	Wipe underneath tables & legs	MS	1/6
10. Dispose of trash (replace bag in receptacle)	X	X	X	X	X	Wipe chair backs and legs	MS	1/6
11. Wipe outside of all cans & lids with disinfectant	X	X	X	X	X	Wipe off cubbies/shelves	MS	1/7
12. Repeat 10 & 11 for diaper pails	X	X	X	X	X	**Immediate Project**		
13. Clean & disinfect high chairs/tables/chairs	X	X	X	X	X	Any surface area contaminated with body fluids such as blood, stool, mucus, vomit, or urine	MS	1/6
14. Clean & disinfect baby beds/cots	X	X	X	X	X			
15. Reduce clutter! (Organize!)	X	X	X	X	X	**Carpet Cleaning – Quarterly**		
16. (infant & toddler groups) Wipe/sanitize toys after each individual use	X	X	X	X	X			
17. Change crib sheets as directed	X	X	X	X	X			
18.								

Lead Teacher: _Ms. Smith_

C – Complete   N/A – Not Applicable

FIGURE 2–8 Cleaning Schedule

REFERENCES

Fuhler, C. J. (2000). *Teaching reading with multicultural books kids love.* Golden, CO: Fulcrum.

Harrington, C. O. (Producer). (1994). *ABC Primetime. From the beginning: Your child's brain* [Television broadcast]. Los Angeles: American Production.

RECOMMENDED RESOURCES

American Society for Testing and Materials (ASTM), http://www.astm.org

Bredekamp, S., & Copple, C. (1997). *Developmentally appropriate practice* (Rev. ed.). Washington, DC: National Association for the Education of Young Children.

Clifford, R. M., Cryer, D., & Harms, T. (1990). *Infant/toddler environment rating scale.* New York: Teachers College Press.

Hall, N. S. (1999). *Creative resources for the anti-bias classroom.* Clifton Park, NY: Thomson Delmar Learning.

Healy, J. M. (1994). *Your child's growing mind* (Rev. ed.). New York: Dell Publishing. (Orignal work published 1987)

National Program for Playground Safety (NPPS), http://www.playgroundsafety.org

Paashe, C. L., Gorrill, L., & Strom, B. (2004). *Children with special seeds in early childhood settings.* Clifton Park, NY: Thomson Delmar Learning.

HELPFUL WEB SITE

Roper, T. (2001). *Brain scan technology.* http://www.unt.edu

MORE RESOURCES FOR SCHOOL SUPPLIES AND EQUIPMENT

Constructive Playthings, 13201 Arrington Road, Grandview, MO 64030-2886, 1-800-448-4115, http://www.cptoys.com

Kaplan Early Learning Company, P. O. Box 609, Lewisville, NC 27023-0609, 1-800-334-2014, http://www.kaplanco.com

United Art and Education, P. O. Box 9219, Fort Wayne, IN 46899, 1-800-322-3247, http://www.unitednow.com

3

Establishing an Excellent Path for Ongoing Communication

To find your specific State's Licensing, Rules and Regulations go to:

http://nrc.uchsc.edu

INDIVIDUAL KIDEX "BABY BOOKS"

In today's fast-paced world, little time is available for busy working parents to keep a written record of their child's early years. Although a "baby book" is not necessary, it can serve as a wonderful keepsake. A tremendous amount of written data is accumulated over the course of caring for little ones. Consider collecting the important pieces and assembling a "baby book" for each child (see Figure 3–1).

Begin with a binder with a clear-view front, which can be found in any office supply store. Use the cover template (see Figure 3–2 for an example), cheerful infant stationery, or paper with your center's logo to create the front cover. Use this binder to store the completed "Baby's Monthly Profile" sheets, "Developmental Milestones" sheet, "Planned Activity" sheets, photos, and newsletters. There are numerous possibilities for constructing an individual baby book.

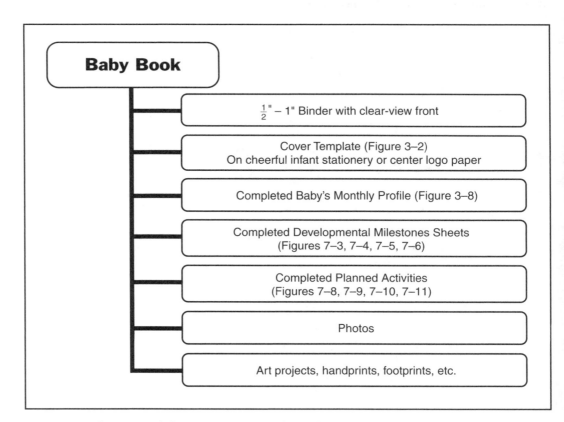

FIGURE 3–1 Suggested Components for a Baby Book

KIDEX
for
INFANTS

Annie

BABY'S NAME

200x

YEAR

FIGURE 3–2 KIDEX for Infants Book Cover

Share the information with the parents or guardians as it is collected, and place it in the baby book in the baby's cubby or locker for their periodic review; then keep it in the infant room all year and present it to the parents on the baby's first birthday.

Some states require that such written information be kept in each child's permanent record. In that case, it might be helpful to create duplicate copies, one to follow the baby to the next care group and one to share with the family. The family book will contain more personalized keepsakes such as photos and mementos collected along the way. This treasure is worth all the extra effort: not only will the family enjoy it for years to come, you will also promote your program. A great deal of time is spent planning and caring for infants every day. When a "baby book" is completed, your efforts are visible!

KIDEX FOR INFANTS CLASS BOOK

Create a KIDEX for Infants Class Book, and place this book in a central location to house information important for the whole group. The KIDEX Class Book is similar to an operating manual for each individual group. Pertinent information stored in this book will help guide substitute teachers with providing continuous care in your absence. Collect information such as the daily infant room schedule, nutrition schedules (if space does not allow for a nutrition board on the wall), emergency postings and procedures, future planned events, educational articles, meeting minutes, and other pertinent information a substitute would find helpful. If resources are limited, you can eliminate the individual baby books and use the KIDEX Class Book to include all the individual infants' information as well. Place the KIDEX Class Book in a visible location so the substitute caregiver or program personnel can find it at a moment's notice if you are absent or unavailable. The KIDEX Class Book can also serve as a valuable reference at program meetings.

HOW TO ASSEMBLE A KIDEX CLASS BOOK

Figure 3–3 shows an example of a cover for the class book. A template is also available in the Forms and Templates Appendix at the back of the book. Figure 3–4 provides a flowchart for creating the KIDEX Class Book. Purchase a binder, preferably one that has a clear-view front and enough index tabs to create as many sections as you will need in the book. Along with each section on the flowchart are the specific figure numbers that will help you locate examples and blank templates. Organize your KIDEX Class Book into sections as indicated on the flowchart. It is a good idea to ask a colleague to review your book in order to verify whether the written instructions reflect your intentions.

INFANT ROOM ENROLLING APPLICATION

Begin building a file for each new infant. Items to include on an application for collecting general information are:

infant's name, address, home phone number, date of birth, gender, legal guardian
mother's name, address, home phone number, employer's name, work phone number
father's name, address, home phone number, employer's name, work phone number
emergency contact's name, relationship, address, home phone number, work phone number

KIDEX *for* INFANTS
Class Book

Blueberries

GROUP NAME

FIGURE 3–3 KIDEX Class Book Cover

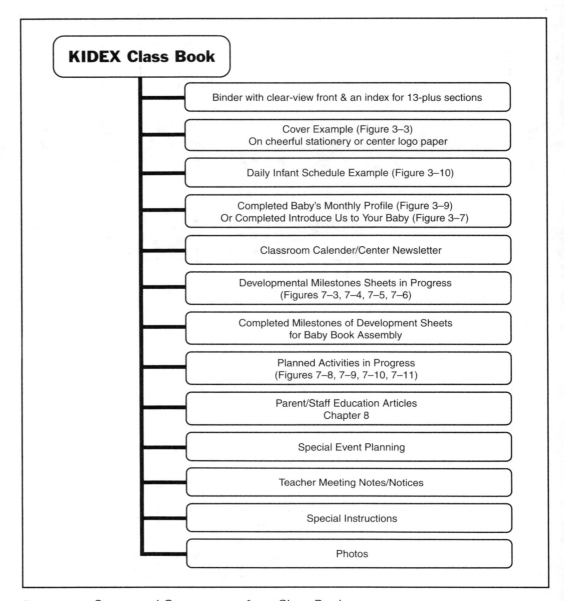

FIGURE 3–4 Suggested Components for a Class Book

names of other people residing with the baby, their relationship, age (if under 21)

names of all people authorized to remove the infant from the infant room, relationships

days the baby will attend, full or part time

medical emergency information and authorization

permission to leave the infant room for neighborhood walks, bus ride to and from the center, etc. (see Figure 3–5).

INFANT ROOM ENROLLING APPLICATION

Child's Full Name: _Jamae (Enter Last Name)_ Nickname _Jamae, Bear_

Date of Birth: _10/30/08_ Sex: _M_ Home Phone: _xxx-xxx-xxxx_

Address: _(Enter Street #/Apt. #)_ City: _(Enter City)_ Zip Code: _(Enter Zip Code)_

Legal Guardian: _Ms. Rust_

Mother's Name: _Ms. Rust_ Home Phone: _xxx-xxx-xxxx_

Address: _(Enter Street #/Apt. #)_ City: _(Enter City)_ Zip Code: _(Enter Zip Code)_

Employer: _St. Joseph's Hospital_ Work Phone: _xxx-xxx-xxxx_

Address: _(Enter Street #/Apt. #)_ City: _(Enter City)_ Zip Code: _(Enter Zip Code)_

Father's Name: _Mr. Jackson_ Home Phone: _xxx-xxx-xxxx_

Address: _(Enter Street #/Apt. #)_ City: _(Enter City)_ Zip Code: _(Enter Zip Code)_

Employer: _John Deere & Associates_ Work Phone: _xxx-xxx-xxxx_

Address: _(Enter Street #/Apt. #)_ City: _(Enter City)_ Zip Code: _(Enter Zip Code)_

IN THE EVENT YOU CANNOT BE REACHED IN AN EMERGENCY, CALL:

Name: _Ms. Rust_ Relationship: _Grandmother_ Phone: _xxx-xxx-xxxx_

Address: _(Enter Street #/Apt. #)_ City: _(Enter City)_ Zip Code: _(Enter Zip Code)_

Name: _Ms. Jackson_ Relationship: _Grandmother_ Phone: _xxx-xxx-xxxx_

Address: _(Enter Street #/Apt. #)_ City: _(Enter City)_ Zip Code: _(Enter Zip Code)_

OTHER PEOPLE RESIDING WITH BABY

Name: _Rodney (Enter Last Name)_ Relationship: _Brother_ Age: _7_

Name: _Dwight (Enter Last Name)_ Relationship: _Brother_ Age: _6_

Name: _Sara (Enter Last Name)_ Relationship: _Sister_ Age: _3_

FIGURE 3–5 Infant Enrolling Application example

PEOPLE AUTHORIZED TO REMOVE BABY FROM THE NURSERY

Your baby will not be allowed to go with anyone unless their name appears on this application, or you provide them with an "authorization card," or you make other arrangements with the management. Positive I.D. will be required.

Name: _Ms. Rust_ Relationship: _Mother_

Name: _Mr. Jackson_ Relationship: _Father_

Name: _Ms. Rust_ Relationship: _Grandmother_

Baby Will Attend: (Mon) - Tues - (Wed) - Thur - (Fri) Sat - Sun

Baby Will Be: (Full Time) or Part Time

Time Child Will Be Dropped Off (Normally): _8:00 am_

Time Child Will Be Picked Up (Normally): _4:30 pm_

MEDICAL INFORMATION/AUTHORIZATION

Physician's Name: _Dr. Gillespie_ Phone: _xxx-xxx-xxxx_

Address: _(Enter Street #/Apt. #)_ City: _(Enter City)_ Zip Code: _(Enter Zip Code)_

Dentist's Name: _Dr. Cooper_ Phone: _xxx-xxx-xxxx_

Address: _(Enter Street #/Apt. #)_ City: _(Enter City)_ Zip Code: _(Enter Zip Code)_

Allergies: _None Known_

I agree and give consent that, in case of accident, injury, or illness of a serious nature, my child will be given medical attention/emergency care. I understand I will be contacted immediately, or as soon as possible if I am away from the numbers listed on this form.

PERMISSION TO LEAVE PREMISES

I hereby give the nursery _Somersett Heights_ permission to take my child on

neighborhood walks using a _baby buggy_ (state equipment, e.g., a baby

buggy that seats six children & has safety straps). YES _NR_ (INITIAL)

NO, I do not give permission at this time: _____ (INITIAL)

Parent/Guardian's Signature: _Ms. Rust_

Parent/Guardian's Signature: _Mr. Jackson_

Date: _04/01/2009_

Figure 3–5 Infant Enrolling Application example *(Continued)*

AUTHORIZED
PERSON
CARD

USE HEAVY CARD STOCK (FRONT OF CARD)

Reverend James
Name of Authorized Person

May pick up my child Joseph

on my behalf.

3/16/xx

Parent/Guardian Signature   Date

USE HEAVY CARD STOCK (BACK OF CARD)

FIGURE 3–6 Authorization Card (Front & Back)

IMMUNIZATIONS

To protect all children attending the center, medical authorities suggest they all have current immunizations. Since the recommended dosages and types of immunizations continually fluctuate, you can refer to the American Academy of Pediatrics Web site (http://www.aap.org) or your local health department for the most recent schedule. Sometimes a center encounters children who do not have current immunizations for a variety of reasons such as medical conditions or religious preferences. If immunizations are withheld for any reason, collect in writing from the parent or legal guardian, the child's physician, and/or religious leader the specific reason and keep it in the child's record. Special care should be taken to notify and exclude underimmunized children from the program if an active vaccine-preventable disease occurs in the facility.

The Infant Room Enrolling Application template mentions "authorization cards" under "People Authorized to Remove Baby from the Nursery" (see Figure 3–6). Consider using authorization cards for those occasions when parents/guardians are unable to remove their baby from the nursery due to unforeseen circumstances. They might need to depend on a substitute such as a coworker, neighbor, or family member not on the authorized list. Upon enrollment, provide the family with a couple of blank authorization cards. Instruct them to complete one and call the infant room to give verbal permission and provide the name of the person who will call for the baby. Some states require a code number or word to accompany the authorized person. Check your local licensing agency for specific password mandates. When the substitute person arrives, request a picture I.D. to verify that the name matches the one on the authorization card. Collect the card and return it to the parents.

INTRODUCE US TO YOUR BABY

When an infant is enrolled in your infant room, provide the parents/guardians with an "Introduce Us to Your Baby" sheet (Figure 3–7). This form is used to gather information to quickly familiarize the caregiving staff with that particular infant's needs and requirements. Once the baby has been in attendance this document should be replaced monthly with updated information. The replacement document is the "Baby's Monthly Profile," illustrated in Figure 3–8.

Introduce Us to Your Baby

Baby's Name: _Stacy (Enter Last Name)_   Nickname: _____   Date of Birth: _10/30/79_

Father's Name: _Mr. Callaway_   Mother's Name: _Mrs. Callaway_

Siblings' Names & Ages: _Stephanie   3 years old, Courtney   5 years old_

SLEEPING PATTERNS:

1. How does your baby show you he or she is ready for sleep? _She rubs eyes & yawns_

2. How do you prepare baby for nap? (rocking, swinging, etc.) _Rocking_

Time	Napping Approx. how long?	Time	Indicate Food & Formula
10:30 am	1 hour	7:00 am	5-8 oz formula 2-3 T Baby cereal
2:00 pm	2 1/2 hour	9:00 am	5-8 oz formula 5 oz Water
Bedtime 7:00 pm		12:00 Noon	5-8 oz formula 1/2 any toast or 2 crackers
		3:00 pm	5-8 oz formula 8 oz Water
		6:00 pm	5 oz Water 2-3 T Baby cereal

EATING PATTERNS:

1. Name of formula currently using: _Similac_

2. Are you currently breast-feeding? _Only at night_

3. What type of bottles and nipples do you use? _Gerber bottles & nipples_

4. Do you feed your baby water? If so, how often? _Yes, After drinking formula if still thirsty_

5. Are there any eating difficulties? _Needs burping after she completes formula_

6. Has your baby started cereal? If yes, how often and how much? _4 T w/strained fruit breakfast_

7. Does your baby have any allergies? _None known_

8. Do you wish for your baby to feed on demand? _Yes_

9. Does your baby take a pacifier? _No_   Type: _____

10. How does your baby indicate he or she is hungry? _She becomes fussy and cries_

11. Do you have any nutrition concerns we should be aware of? _None known_

FIGURE 3–7 Introduce Us to Your Baby example

ELIMINATION PATTERNS:

1. How often do you change your baby's diaper at home? _10–12 x a day_

2. How frequently does your baby eliminate B.M. stools? _1–3 x a day_

3. What is the usual color or consistency of the stool? _Mustard yellow_

HEALTH PATTERNS:

1. Does your baby regularly take medications? _No, only vitamins_ If yes, please indicate the type, amount, and time it is given: _____

2. Are there any health problems or handicaps? _No_ If yes, please state specifically:
    _____

ACTIVITY PATTERNS:

At what age did your child begin creeping? _Not yet_ crawling? _____ walking? _____

STRESS/COPING PATTERNS:

Describe your baby's teething symptoms: _Not yet_
Is there any other information we should know that will help us get acquainted with your baby?

She has begun to flip and turn over. Please watch carefully.
_____
_____
_____
_____
_____

List all names of people authorized to take your baby from the center: _Mr. Callaway_
_____

Baby will attend: (MON) TUE (WED) THUR (FRI) SAT SUN Start Date: _3/1_

Time baby will normally arrive: _8:00 am_ depart: _3:00 am_
Person completing interview: _Ms. Smith_
Parent / Guardian Signature: _Mrs. Callaway_
Parent / Guardian Signature: _Mr. Callaway_

In order to assure a smooth transition, this completed form must accompany baby when care is initiated.

Figure 3–7 Introduce Us to your Baby example *(Continued)*

CURRENT EVENTS BULLETIN BOARD

Hang a bulletin board near the infant room entrance. In a busy infant room time is of the essence. Create a bulletin board seasonally so you don't have to spend time changing it more than a few times a year. The bulletin board will promote communication between your program, current participating families, and future families touring your facility. Suggested key components are:

Daily Infant Room Schedule:	Use this area to post the general schedule for the whole group (Figure 3–10).
Birthdays:	Post the birth date of each infant.
Coming Up:	Here is a great place to post future events: for example, Muscular Distrophy Association MDA, fund-raising, jump-a-thon (using a baby jumper).
Infant Room News:	Post current events such as who took his or her first step or has a new tooth, or family news (a new baby brother is on the way!).
Health News:	Choose articles from Chapter 8 to explain a recent exposure to a communicable disease.
Parent Education:	Post information relevant to infants, such as ways to prevent Sudden Infant Death Syndrome, or parenting class offerings in the community.
Calendars:	If your center creates a monthly newsletter or calendar, post current copies here.

BABY'S MONTHLY PROFILE

It is amazing how much a baby changes in a four-week period. Accurate and updated information is crucial to ensure a baby's care matches his or her current needs. The Baby's Monthly Profile provides a place to record each infant's preferences and routines (see Figure 3–8). A blank template can be found in the Forms and Templates Appendix. Baby's Monthly Profile replaces Introduce Us to Your Baby, initially completed by the parents. Complete a Baby's Monthly Profile for each infant and update it monthly. Although this might seem time-consuming, it actually is very easy and quick because you are now very familiar with a baby's routines. On this sheet, provide individualized information and instructions for each baby. Write clear and concise instructions and information to help another teacher develop a quick understanding of the baby's needs in your absence. Remember that others often do not have the relationship you have established with the baby and are not as familiar with all the important details. Record the baby's average nap length and frequency, and whether he or she has a special routine that helps him or her fall asleep. For example, some babies love to be rocked whereas others enjoy music. What is the baby's normal activity level? What type of formula does he or she use? What type of bottle? Are there any specific feeding instructions? Does the baby have any medical needs or skin sensitivities? Does he or she enjoy a pacifier? Do the parents have any special requests or concerns? For example, parents might request that their baby wear a hat outdoors all year round.

BABY'S MONTHLY PROFILE

Month: _Aug 05_   Caregivers: _Ms. Smith_   _Ms. Howard_

Baby's name: _Daniella (Enter Last Name)_ Birth date: _2/10/05_   Age: _5 months_

Parents'/Guardians' names: _____Mrs. Mondragon & Mr. Mondragon_____

Personality Traits: shy/reserved   (outgoing/curious)   sensitive/frightens easily
(Circle all that apply)   very verbal   (active)   restless
    (cuddly)   demonstrative   stranger anxiety
    cautious

Parent's Concerns/Instructions: _____wear hat when outdoors_____

Health Concerns: _____none known_____

Daily Medications: yes _____   no __✓__ (see med sheet for details)

Allergies: _____talcum powder_____

Ointment Used: _Desitin as directed by parents_____

Special Nap Instructions: _she likes fluffy blue bear & pat her back until asleep_____

Usual Nap times _10:30 am_ to _11:30 am_   _2:00 pm_ to _4:00 pm_

Pacifier Type: _____Nuk_____   Bottle/Nipple Type: _____Gerber/Gerber_____

Formula Name: _____Similac_____   Amount: _____5–8oz_____

Baby's Eating Schedule:

Breakfast	Snack/Beverage	Lunch	Snack/Beverage	Dinner	Snack/Beverage
7:00 am	9:00 am	12:00 pm	3:00 pm	6:00 pm	7:30 pm
5–8oz Formula	5–8oz F&W	2–3 T Cereal	5–8 Formula	2–3 T Cereal	5–8oz F & W

Days Attending: (Mon)   Tue   (Wed)   Thur   (Fri)   Sat   Sun

Approx. Arrival: _8:00 am_   Approx. Departure: _4:30 pm_

Those authorized to pick up: _____Mrs. & Mr. Mondragon_____

Warning: If name is not listed, consult with office and obtain permission to release child. If you are not familiar with this person, always request I.D.

FIGURE 3–8 Baby's Monthly Profile example

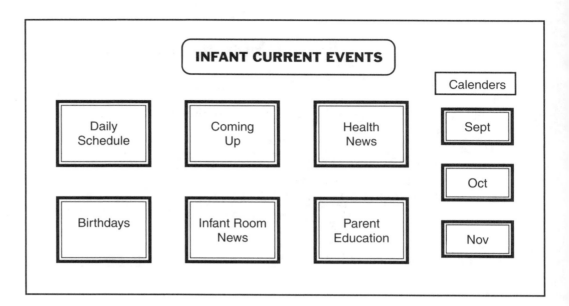

FIGURE 3–9 Infant Current Events Board

DAILY INFANT ROOM SCHEDULE

Post an infant room schedule on the Current Events Bulletin Board and in your centrally located KIDEX Class Book (see Figure 3–10). Parents seeking future care are steady visitors in infant rooms. The information found on the Daily Infant Room Schedule will give them a general idea of what a day is like in the infant room. An empty template is provided in the Forms and Templates Appendix to create your own Daily Infant Room Schedule. This schedule will also help any substitute or part-time teachers provide a consistent day in your absence. Of course, every infant is an individual and even the best planned schedules will need to allow for babies' individual needs and demands.

INFANT DAILY OBSERVATION SHEETS

Keep a written daily record for each infant. Accurate recording in a timely manner gives the family a clear understanding of the baby's day. Adopting a routine for recording ensures all-important aspects are covered. Some infant rooms are busier than others, and some caregivers find checklist observations more convenient. Two methods of record keeping are illustrated in Figures 3–11 and 3–12. Use two-part forms for your daily observation sheets. Provide one for the parents/guardians at departure. File the second copy for at least a couple of months, or longer if your state requires it. Occasionally parents/guardians express concerns: for example, how often a baby's diapers are changed. Some families change diapers more often and others less. It is very helpful to have written observation documents to review if a conference is warranted. These documents arm you with the

Daily Infant Schedule

Early Morning	Arrivals Assist with separation Assign primary caregivers Diaper change (if needed) Baby hand washing Health assessment, check and plan for special instructions or medication needs Breakfast
Mid Morning	Clean up, wash face & hands Inside play (see suggested activities) Diaper change (if didn't change upon arrival) Baby hand washing Morning bottle (formula or juice) Morning nap Diaper change after nap
Late Morning	Outside play (weather permitting) or Stroller walks or baby swing
Mid Day	Hand washing Lunch feeding Clean up from lunch Diaper change Medication as indicated
Early Afternoon	Afternoon nap time Prepare for afternoon activities Update charting Notes home
Mid Afternoon	Wake up Diaper change Baby cleanup/handwashing Bottleand/orsnack
Late Afternoon	Inside play (see suggested activities) Diaper change Baby face and hand washing Change soiled clothing Comb/brush hair Medications as indicated Flooractivities Review charts Gather baby's items to send home
Early Evening	Departures occurring Rocking/singing Bottle, juice or predinner snack Departure

FIGURE 3–10 Daily Infant Schedule example

Infant Daily Observation Checklist

Infant's name: _Grace (Enter Last Name)_   Date: _12-15-2005_

Arrival: _7:30 am_   Departure: _5:40 pm_

	Time	Ate Partial	Ate Complete	Oz Juice	Oz Water	Oz Breast Milk	Oz Formula	Cereal	Fruits	Meat/ Protein	Vegetable	Crackers/ Bread	Initials
Breakfast	7:30		✓	2 oz				✓	✓				H.S.
Snack	11:00					7 oz							KL.
Lunch	12:00 1:15	✓				8 oz			✓		✓✓		JB. KL.
Snack	3:30	✓										✓	KL.
Dinner	5:00				8 oz								JB.
Snack													

Nap Times: _8:35 am – 10:20 am_   _1:40 pm – 2:55 pm_   _____ _____

Diaper Changes				
Time	**Wet**	**BM**	**Dry**	**Initials**
8:00	✓	✓		KL.
10:30	✓			KL.
12:30	✓			JB.
3:00	✓			KL.
4:50			✓	KL.

	Medications*	Treatments*
Time	None	8:00 am Salve
Time		12:30 pm Salve
Time		

*See Daily Medication Sheet for Details

Moods / Activity Level:
Circle all that apply
(Busy) • (Curious) • Adventurous
Cheerful • Quiet • Content • Cuddly
Drowsy • Bubbly • (Verbal/Babbling)
Periods of Fussiness • Grumpy

Comments: _Diaper rash better with_

_____ _new diaper salve_ _____

_____

_____

_____

Primary Caregiver: _Ms. Love_   Shift Time: _8 – 5 pm_

Caregiver: _Mr. Best_   Shift Time: _9 – 6 pm_

Figure 3–11 Infant Daily Observation Checklist example

INFANT DAILY OBSERVATION SHEET

	WET-BM		
Arrival Time: 8:00 am			
		Chasing Ms. Amy	
		2:15 Climbing on Ms. Amy	
6:30	✓ AK	2:30	
		Playing in toy box	
		next to Brian	
7:30		3:30 Rocking w/ Ms. Janine	
		3:45 Bottle 7 oz	
8:00 Juice 2 oz	✓ MH	4:00 Asleep	
Fed cereal/bananas			
8:30 Talking with Ms. Michelle		4:30	
Playing on Floor w/toys			
9:30 Crawling on Floor	✓ MH	5:30	
exploring			
10:05 Bottle 8 oz	✓	5:45 Awake	
10:30	✓ MH	6:00	✓ MH
10:40 Asleep		**Comments:** Kathryn was very hungry at every meal. She must be growing.	
11:30			
12:15 Awake	✓ MH		
12:30 Lunch: Beef, Beets, Applesauce			
Practiced pull ups			
1:20 drank juice 4 oz		**Departure Time:** 6:40 pm	
1:30 Crawling, looking in mirror			

Baby's Name Kathryn (Enter Last Name)

Date 4/21/06   M T W TH F S S

Primary Caregiver Ms. Hart

INFANT DAILY OBSERVATION SHEET

	WET-BM		WET-BM
Arrival Time: 7:00 am		1:40 Asleep	
6:30		2:30	MH Dry
7:00 Playing w/toys		3:00 Awake	
7:30 Oatmeal & peaches		3:30 Crackers, Bottle 8 oz	
		Playing in toy pit	
8:00 Apple juice 2 oz	✓ MH	Banging toys	
Crawling around			
8:30		4:30	✓ MH
8:35 Asleep		Grandma visiting	
		Playing pat-a-cake	
9:30		5:30 Looking in mirror	
		Smiling at Mom	
10:30 Awake	✓ MH	6:00	
Bottle 7 oz		**Comments:** Bob was very cheerful today. We enjoyed his laughter and giggles. Grandma brought out the smiles.	
Chewing on keys			
11:30 Talking w/Megan			
Lunch: Beets, Green Beans, Plums	✓ DS		
Walking around			
12:30			
Dancing to music beat!			
Laughing			
1:30 Bottle 8 oz		**Departure Time:** 5:40 pm	

Baby's Name Bob (Enter Last Name)

Date 4/21/06   M T W TH F S S

Primary Caregiver Ms. Hart

FIGURE 3–12 Infant Daily Observation Sheet example

WRITTEN CHARTING SUGGESTIONS

Write at least one observation every half hour.

Prior to feeding *always* write "Bottle ___ oz." Fill in the amount consumed when bottle is finished. This method will prevent your forgetting to enter the amount if you get too busy.

Write descriptive observations of the baby's activities such as:

- Playing with
- Talking to
- Thinking about
- Pulling up
- Rolling over
- Rolling around
- Zooming around
- Watching
- Singing
- Playing w/gym
- Cuddling
- Rocking with Miss Jill
- Exploring toes

Record when the baby fell asleep and when the baby awakened.

Example: 10:20 Asleep
            11:40 Awake

Always change the baby's diaper upon waking and at least every two hours. Record this information.

Review charts often throughout your shift. When a diaper is changed, chart it.

Review before you leave for lunch and/or at the end of the day. Check the chart for accuracy.

When the nursery is quiet, *chart/review.*

Record on the chart *before* giving a bottle and *after* they eat solids. For instance, draw a line and indicate ounces yet to be consumed: ___ oz. Later fill in the appropriate amount so recording isn't likely to be overlooked. Make it your routine!

When you change the baby's clothing record it: "12:00 Clothing changed due to loose BM or soiled when eating." *Rinse* clothing in water only, cover it in plastic, and put it with the baby's personal items to go home.

If the baby refuses a bottle, *chart it* and try again 30 minutes later.

If the baby's dry at diaper change, *chart it* and check again 30 minutes later.

Fill out first and last names and the date on the chart. Avoid confusion, especially if there are two infants or caregivers with the same name.

Write "Home" when the baby leaves.

FIGURE 3–13 Written Charting Suggestions

information needed to answer a family's concerns and reach an agreeable outcome. The director/lead teacher is encouraged to review all records at least monthly to look for consistent recording practices or spot areas in which intervention or education is warranted.

Record at least one activity every half hour (see Figure 3–13 for written charting suggestions). Prior to feeding, always write "Bottle," followed by a blank line. Fill in the amount consumed when the feeding is completed. This way you won't forget to enter this vital information if you become too busy. Make this a routine. If the baby refuses a bottle, then chart it and try again in 30 minutes.

Write descriptive observations of the baby's activities such as, "Patty is playing with . . . ," "talking to . . . ," "thinking about . . . ," "pulling up," "rolling over" "rolling around," "zooming around," "watching . . . ," "singing," "playing with the gym," "cuddling," "rocking with Miss Lois," "exploring her toes." Always record when the baby fell asleep and woke up. For example: "10:20 a.m. Asleep" and "11:40 a.m. Awake." Write the information clearly. Always change a baby's diaper upon waking and at least every two to three hours. Record whether it was a bowel movement, wet, or dry. If the baby is dry, chart this and check again in 30 minutes. Indicate if any rashes are observed. If the baby's clothes are changed, record this on the chart: "12:00 noon clothes changed due to loose BM" or "soiled when eating."

When the infant room is quiet, catch up on any charting and review. *Before you leave for lunch or at the end of your shift, check the charts for accuracy. Remember: after your shift ends your observations and information provide pertinent information for parent questions and the baby's care. An accurate record is essential!*

HANDLING NOTES SENT HOME/STAFF COLLABORATION

The director/lead teacher is responsible for the overall well-being of the staff, parents, and children. The director/lead teacher must be kept informed of any unusual changes, challenges, or problems that might occur during the course of the shift. It can be very disconcerting for a director/lead teacher to be completely uninformed when an upset client approaches him or her. Discuss any written communication with the director/lead teacher prior to sending notes home, other than a note to request personal supplies or the baby's daily record. After discussing the problem at hand you can devise a shared plan of action. Sharing your concerns with the director/lead teacher will facilitate problem solving as well as keep him or her continually informed. The director may have encountered a similar situation before and have a workable solution.

RECOMMENDED RESOURCES

Caring for our children: National health & safety performance standards (2nd ed.), http://www.ncr.edu

High/Scope Educational Research Foundation, http://www.highscope.org

Shelov, S. P., MD, FAAP, & Hannemann, R. E., MD, FAAP. *Caring for your baby and young child: Birth to age 5* (4th ed.), by American Academy of Pediatrics, http://www.aap.org

CHAPTER

To find your specific
State's Licensing, Rules
and Regulations go to:

http://nrc.uchsc.edu

Hygiene, Cleaning, and Disinfecting

Proper cleaning, disinfecting, and hygiene practices employed consistently in an early care and teaching environment will significantly reduce the spread of infection and disease. Disinfecting and cleaning are two distinctly different procedures used to prevent the spread of germs and require their own specific measures to achieve their intended results. *Cleaning* is a *less* rigorous procedure and is designed to remove dirt, soil, and small amounts of bacteria. It *does not eliminate all germs*. Soap, detergents, and cleaners are examples of cleaning products. *Disinfecting* procedures are *more* rigorous and refer to cleaning surfaces with the use of chemicals, *virtually eliminating all germs*. Diaper tables are an example of a place where disinfecting procedures are employed. In order for a disinfectant solution to work effectively, the instructions must be adhered to. Disinfecting products require a certain concentration of solution and must remain in contact with the contaminated item for a specific period of time. The Environmental Protection Agency (EPA) regulates the use of disinfectants. To avoid confusing a cleaning agent with a disinfecting agent, look at the label. Products that are capable of disinfecting will bear an EPA approval on the label.

If you are mixing your own disinfecting solutions, the National Health and Safety Performance Standards for Child Care recommends ¼ cup of bleach in 1 gallon of water. Mix fresh daily. To avoid creating a poisonous gas, never mix bleach with anything other than water.

Chlorine bleach solutions have been known to aggravate asthma or other respiratory conditions. Some care providers are concerned with the potential toxic effects of common household products used abundantly in an early care environment. There are several effective natural disinfecting products on the market. Check your local health food stores for a variety of products or check in the recommended resources section at the end of this chapter.

CLEAN FOOTWEAR POLICY

Infants spend a great deal of time creeping, crawling, and playing on the floor in the infant room. Nurseries experience an overabundance of foot traffic in a given day. Consider adopting a clean footwear policy in your infant room. Removing street shoes upon entering the infant room can greatly reduce surface dirt, bacteria, and germs. The staff will need to keep a pair of "infant room only shoes" or nonskid socks to wear inside the infant room only. Encourage staff, parents, and visitors to remove their street footwear, wear shoe covers, or stand on a designated rug placed very close to the door. Position a chair in a convenient location near the infant room door so visitors can sit while they remove their shoes. Sometimes parents/guardians or visitors are in a hurry and do not have time to change. The designated rug placed near the entrance will serve as a safe area to remain in soiled street-worn shoes. Make it a policy that family members and visitors must remain in this area if removing their shoes is not feasible. Be aware, then, that they will require some assistance with arrival or departure. Parents/guardians will appreciate your efforts to avoid spreading unnecessary dirt in the infants' environment.

DIAPER CHANGING PROCEDURES

Frequent diaper changing ensures a baby's comfort and prevents skin irritations. Diaper changing time is a wonderful opportunity for sharing one-on-one moments. This is a repetitive routine performed many times a day. Opportunities to share a meaningful experience with the child could be missed if care is not taken to be fully present during this time. Use this occasion to listen, talk, or sing with baby. Describe your actions, such as: "Laura, it's now your turn to have a diaper change. A dry diaper will feel so nice!" Plan specific "sharing time" subjects to discuss with the babies, or choose interesting pictures to keep in the diapering area and change them often. Post them near the diaper changing table for all staff to use. Diaper changing can be a very vulnerable time for children, and how we treat them communicates our attitude toward them. They will develop feelings of acceptance and security in a kind and respectful climate.

Always check a baby's diaper status upon arrival. Form the habit of changing babies' diapers after they awaken from a nap and at least every two to three hours as needed. Infants will require at least four or five diaper changes during an eight- to nine-hour shift.

Absolute cleanliness and adherence to consistent standards are vital during diaper changes. Many viruses and infections are easily spread from child to child. A disease can be carried by people who are completely without symptoms and passed on to others causing severe diarrhea to the point of dehydration, hospitalization, and lengthy illness. Employing the outlined procedures each time you change a diaper will ensure that you and the infants will remain healthy (see Figure 4–1 for disposable diaper changing procedures and Figure 4–2 for cloth diaper changing procedures).

The suggested diaper changing equipment and details for creating a diaper changing area are listed in Chapter 1. Requirements for diaper changes vary from state to state. Some areas, for instance, allow changing to occur in the infant's personally assigned crib; others allow a choice of whether disposable gloves are used. According to Standard 3.014 Diaper Changing Procedure *Caring for Our Children, National Health and Safety Performance Standards* (2nd ed.), the following diaper changing procedures should be posted in the changing area and shall be assessed as part of staff evaluation of caregivers who do diaper changing. Caregivers must never leave a child alone on a table or countertop, even for an instant. A safety strap or harness shall not be used on the diaper changing table. If an emergency arises, caregivers shall put the child on the floor or take the child with them.

STEP 1: Get organized. Before you bring the child to the diaper changing area, wash your hands, gather what you need, and bring it to the diaper changing table:

- Nonabsorbent paper liner large enough to cover the changing surface from the child's shoulders to beyond the child's feet.
- Fresh diaper, clean clothes (if you need them).
- Wipes for cleaning the child's genitalia and buttocks—use a pop-up dispenser or remove the wipes from the container so you will not touch the container during diaper changing.
- A plastic bag for any soiled clothes.
- Disposable gloves, if you plan to use them (put gloves on before handling soiled clothing or diapers).
- A thick application of any diaper cream (when appropriate) removed from the container to a piece of disposable material such as facial or toilet tissue.

Diaper Changing Procedures for Disposable Diapers

Supplies: Disposable nonabsorbent gloves, nonabsorbent paper, liner disposable wipes removed from container, child's personally labeled ointments (under medical direction), diapers, cotton balls, plastic bags, tissues, physician-prescribed lotions, lidded hands-free plastic-lined trash container, soap, disinfectant, and paper towels.

Use a nonabsorbent changing surface. Avoid dangerous falls: keep a hand on baby at all times and never leave alone. In emergency, put child on floor or take with you.

	Steps for Changing Disposable Diapers				
1	Wash hands with liquid soap and water.	2	Gather supplies.	3	Put on disposable waterproof gloves (if used).
4	Cover diapering surface with nonabsorbent paper liner.	5	Place baby on prepared diapering area (minimize contact: hold baby away from your body if extremely wet or soiled).	6	Put soiled clothes in a plastic bag.
7	Unfasten diaper. Leave soiled diaper under the child.	8	Gently wash baby's bottom. Remove stool and urine from front to back, and use a fresh wipe each time. Dispose directly in designated receptacle.	9	Fold soiled diaper inward and place in designated receptacle followed by the disposable gloves (if used).
10	Use disposable wipe to clean surface of caregiver's hands and another to clean the child's.	11	Check for spills on paper. If present, fold over so fresh part is under buttocks.	12	Place clean diaper under baby.
13	Using a cotton ball or tissue, apply skin ointment to clean, dry area if indicated/ordered.	14	Fasten diaper and dress with fresh clothing.	15	Wash baby's hands with soap and water between 60°F and 120°F for 15–20 sec. and dry. Turn faucet off with a paper towel, then place baby in a safe location.
16	Clean and disinfect diapering area, leaving bleach solution in contact at least 2 minutes. Allow table to air dry, or wipe it after 2 minutes.	17	Wash your hands with soap and water for at least 15–20 seconds. Turn off faucet with paper towel.	18	Chart diaper change and any observations.

Adapted from: Standard 3.014 Diaper Changing Procedure. *Caring for our children, National health and safety performance standards* (2nd ed.). Used with permission, American Academy of Pediatrics.

FIGURE 4–1 Diaper Changing Procedures for Disposable Diapers

Diaper Changing Procedures for Cloth Diapers

Supplies: Disposable nonabsorbent gloves, nonabsorbent paper liner, disposable wipes removed from container, child's personally labeled ointments (under medical direction), diapers, cotton balls, plastic bags, tissues, physician-prescribed lotions, lidded hands-free plastic-lined trash container, soap, disinfectant, and paper towels.

Soiled Diapers: *Contain in a labeled and washable plastic-lined receptacle that is tightly lidded and hands-free only. Don't require separate bags. However, any soiled diapers sent home are to be secured in a plastic bag, separately bagged from soiled clothing. Clean and disinfect receptacle daily and dispose of waste water in toilet or floor drain only.*

Use a nonabsorbent changing surface. Avoid dangerous falls: keep a hand on baby at all times and never leave alone. In emergency, put child on floor or take with you.

Steps for Changing Cloth Diapers					
1	Wash hands with liquid soap and water.	2	Gather supplies.	3	Put on disposable waterproof gloves (if used).
4	Cover diapering surface with nonabsorbent paper liner.	5	Place baby on prepared diapering area (minimize contact: hold baby away from your body if extremely wet or soiled).	6	Put soiled clothes in a plastic bag.
7	Unfasten diaper. Leave soiled diaper under the child. Close each safety pin immediately out of child's reach. Never hold pins in mouth.	8	Gently wash baby's bottom. Remove stool and urine from front to back, and use a fresh wipe each time. Dispose directly in designated receptacle.	9	Fold soiled diaper inward and place in designated receptacle followed by the disposable gloves (if used).
10	Use disposable wipe to clean surface of caregiver's hands and another to clean the child's.	11	Check for spills on paper. If present, fold over so fresh part is under buttocks.	12	Place clean diaper under baby.
13	Using a cotton ball or tissue, apply skin ointment to clean, dry area if indicated/ordered.	14	Fasten diaper with pins, placing your hand between the child and the diaper on insertion, and dress with fresh clothing.	15	Wash baby's hands with soap and water between 60°F and 120°F for 15–20 sec. and dry. Turn faucet off with a paper towel, then place baby in a safe location.
16	Clean and disinfect diapering area, leaving bleach solution in contact at least 2 minutes. Allow table to air dry, or wipe it after 2 minutes.	17	Wash your hands with soap and water for at least 15–20 seconds. Turn off faucet with paper towel.	18	Chart diaper change and any observations.

Adapted from: Standard 3.014 Diaper Changing Procedure. *Caring for our children, National health and safety performance standards* (2nd ed.). Used with permission, American Academy of Pediatrics.

FIGURE 4–2 Diaper Changing Procedures for Cloth Diapers

STEP 2: Carry the child to the changing table, keeping soiled clothing away from you and any surfaces you cannot easily clean and sanitize after the change.

- Always keep a hand on the child.
- If the child's feet cannot be kept out of the diaper or from contact with soiled skin during the changing process, remove the child's shoes and socks so the child does not contaminate these surfaces with stool or urine during the diaper change.
- Put soiled clothes in a plastic bag and securely tie the plastic bag to send the soiled clothes home.

STEP 3: Clean the child's diaper area.

- Place the child on the diaper changing surface and unfasten the diaper but leave the soiled diaper under the child.
- If safety pins are used, close each pin immediately once it is removed and keep pins out of the child's reach. Never hold pins in your mouth.
- Lift the child's legs as needed to use disposable wipes to clean the skin on the child's genitalia and buttocks. Remove stool and urine from front to back, and use a fresh wipe each time. Put the soiled wipes into the soiled diaper or directly into a plastic-lined, hands-free, covered can.

STEP 4: Remove the soiled diaper without contaminating any surface not already in contact with stool or urine.

- Fold the soiled surface of the diaper inward.
- Put soiled disposable diapers in a covered, plastic-lined, hands-free, covered can. If reusable cloth diapers are used, put the soiled cloth diaper and its contents (without emptying or rinsing) in a plastic bag or into a plastic-lined, hands-free, covered can to give to the parents or laundry service.
- If gloves were used, remove them using the proper technique and put them into a plastic-lined, hands-free, covered can.
- Whether or not gloves were used, use a disposable wipe to clean the surfaces of the caregiver's hands and another to clean the child's hands, and put the wipes into the plastic-lined, hands-free, covered can.
- Check for spills under the child. If there are any, fold over the paper that extends under the child's feet so a fresh, unsoiled paper surface is now under the child's buttocks.

STEP 5: Put on a clean diaper and dress the child.

- Slide a fresh diaper under the child.
- Use a facial or toilet tissue to apply any necessary diaper creams, discarding the tissue in a plastic-lined, hands-free, covered can.
- Note and plan to report any skin problems such as redness, skin cracks, or bleeding.
- Fasten the diaper. If pins are used, place your hand between the child and the diaper when inserting the pin.

STEP 6: Wash the child's hands and return the child to a supervised area.

- Use soap and water, no less than 60°F and no more than 120°F, at a sink to wash the child's hands, if you can.
- If a child is too heavy to hold for hand washing or cannot stand at the sink, use commercial disposable diaper wipes or follow this procedure:

- Wipe the child's hands with a damp paper towel moistened with a drop of liquid soap.
- Wipe the child's hands with a paper towel wet with clear water.
- Dry the child's hands with a paper towel.

STEP 7: Clean and sanitize the diaper changing surface.

- Dispose of the disposable paper liner used on the diaper changing surface in a plastic-lined, hands-free, covered can.
- Clean any visible soil from the changing surface with detergent and water; rinse with water.
- Wet the entire changing surface with the sanitizing solution (i.e., spray a sanitizing solution of ¼ cup of household liquid chlorine bleach in 1 gallon of tap water, mixed fresh daily).
- Put away the spray bottle of sanitizer. If the recommended bleach solution is sprayed as a sanitizer on the surface, leave it in contact with the surface for at least 2 minutes. The surface can be left to air dry or can be wiped dry after 2 minutes of contact with the bleach solution.

STEP 8: Wash your hands, and record the diaper change in the child's daily log.

- In the daily log, record what was in the diaper and any problems (such as a loose stool, an unusual odor, blood in the stool, or any skin irritation); report as necessary.

PRACTICING DIAPER RETURN DEMONSTRATIONS

In a medical setting it is common for the personnel to employ the use of return practice demonstrations for procedures requiring sterile or hygienic techniques. Sterile and hygienic practices must be carried out in a specific order. Cutting corners by leaving out parts of a routine procedure will compromise the integrity of the hygienic practice.

Although most child care programs are not medical programs, the adoption of some of their notable practices makes sense. Diaper changing sessions consume a large part of every day in an infant room. The very nature of repeating a task over and over can become monotonous at times, thus lending itself to a break in procedure. A breakdown in procedure will seriously compromise the hygienic practices necessary for positive health promotion in the infant group.

Adopt the habit of observing all child care personnel perform a return practice demonstration for diapers on a regular basis. Figures 4–3 and 4–4 can be used for an observation record to be used during the return practice procedure. In smaller program settings this could be practiced on a quarterly basis. In larger centers involving a broader range of staffing or one that is experiencing high turnover rates, employ return practice demonstrations once a month. The practice will keep everyone's diaper changing techniques sharp. It will also help shy personnel build their demonstration confidence for those occasional visits and observations conducted by the licensing agencies.

STORING PERSONAL BELONGINGS

If the parents are supplying diapers, request that they provide disposable diapers in unopened packages to ensure proper sanitation is maintained. Avoid storing the diapers on the floor. Store clothing, diapers, and personal items for each infant in an individual

Return Practice Demonstration for Disposable Diapering Procedures

Name: _____Betsy_____   Date: ___7-13___

Observer: _____Miss Carmen_____

Procedure:

___X___   Wash hands with liquid soap and water.

___X___   Gather supplies.

___X___   Put on disposable waterproof gloves (if used).

___X___   Cover diapering surface with nonabsorbent paper liner.

___X___   Place baby on prepared diapering area (minimize contact: hold baby away from your body if extremely wet or soiled).

___X___   Put soiled clothes in a plastic bag.

___X___   Unfasten diaper. Leave soiled diaper under the child.

___X___   Gently wash baby's bottom. Remove stool and urine from front to back, and use a fresh wipe each time. Dispose directly in designated receptacle.

___X___   Fold soiled diaper inward and place in designated receptacle followed by the disposable gloves (if used).

___X___   Use disposable wipe to clean surface of caregiver's hands and another to clean the child's.

___X___   Check for spills on paper. If present, fold over so fresh part is under buttocks.

___X___   Place clean diaper under baby.

___X___   Using a cotton ball or tissue, apply skin ointment to clean, dry area if indicated/ ordered.

___X___   Fasten diaper and dress with fresh clothing.

___X___   Wash baby's hands with soap and water between 60°F and 120°F for 15–20 seconds and dry. Turn faucet off with a paper towel, then place baby in a safe location.

___X___   Clean and disinfect diapering area, leaving bleach solution in contact at least 2 minutes. Allow table to air dry, or wipe it after 2 minutes.

___X___   Wash your hands with soap and water for at least 15–20 seconds. Turn off faucet with paper towel.

___X___   Chart diaper change and any observations.

FIGURE 4–3 Return Practice Demonstration for Disposable Diapering Procedures

Return Practice Demonstration for Cloth Diapering Procedures

Name: _____*Derek*_____   Date: _*7-13*___

Observer: _____*Ms. Stanley*_____

Procedure:

___X___   Wash hands with liquid soap and water.

___X___   Gather supplies.

___X___   Put on disposable waterproof gloves (if used).

___X___   Cover diapering surface with nonabsorbent paper liner.

___X___   Place baby on prepared diapering area (minimize contact: hold baby away from your body if extremely wet or soiled).

___X___   Put soiled clothes in a plastic bag.

___X___   Unfasten diaper. Leave soiled diaper under the child. Close each safety pin immediately out of child's reach. Never hold pins in mouth.

___X___   Gently wash baby's bottom. Remove stool and urine from front to back, and use a fresh wipe each time. Dispose directly in designated receptacle.

___X___   Fold soiled diaper inward and place in designated receptacle followed by the disposable gloves (if used).

___X___   Use disposable wipe to clean surface of caregiver's hands and another to clean the child's.

___X___   Check for spills on paper. If present, fold over so fresh part is under buttocks.

___X___   Place clean diaper under baby.

___X___   Using a cotton ball or tissue, apply skin ointment to clean, dry area if indicated/ordered.

___X___   Fasten diaper with pins, placing your hand between the child and the diaper on insertion, and dress with fresh clothing.

___X___   Wash baby's hands with soap and water between 60°F and 120°F for 15–20 seconds and dry. Turn faucet off with a paper towel, then place baby in a safe location.

___X___   Clean and disinfect diapering area, leaving bleach solution in contact at least 2 minutes. Allow table to air dry, or wipe it after 2 minutes.

___X___   Wash your hands with soap and water for at least 15–20 seconds. Turn off faucet with paper towel.

___X___   Chart diaper change and any observations.

FIGURE 4–4 Return Practice Demonstration for Cloth Diapering Procedures

container, cubby, or locker. Do not allow one infant's personal belongings to touch another infant's. This habit will reduce the potential cross-contamination of other children's personal items from germs or infestation, by head lice (pediculosis) or scabies, for instance.

HANDLING WET AND SOILED CLOTHING

When an infant's clothing becomes wet or soiled, remove the soiled item and replace it with something clean and dry. If the item is extremely soiled with food, rinse it out in cool water only so the stain will not set; then place it in a plastic bag, secure it, and store it in a place for the parents to find at the time of departure. If it is soiled with feces or urine *do not* rinse it; just place it directly in a plastic bag and securely close it. In order to ensure the clothing is not damaged or misplaced, do not launder any of the soiled clothing you take off of a baby. Each parent has his or her own personal way of laundering clothing. To avoid mildewed clothing or permanent stains, send items home promptly. To prevent future misunderstandings when items are returned to families, share this policy and its rationale with them at the time of enrollment.

HAND WASHING PROCEDURES

Frequent hand washing is a cornerstone for a healthy early care and education program. Proper hand washing prevents the spread of many communicable diseases such as E. coli contamination (found in large proportion in feces), hepatitis, giardia, pinworms, and a host of many more common ailments. All are spread via fecal–oral route from anus to mouth.

Giardiasis and pinworms are the two most common parasitic infections among children in the United States.

Wong (1999) found "the incidence of intestinal parasitic disease, especially giardiasis, has increased among young children who attend daycare centers" (p. 736). "Hand washing is the single most effective and critical measure and control of hepatitis in any setting" (p. 1577).

Your best defense for reducing the spread of illness lies in consistent hand washing habits. Hand washing for staff and children is recommended before and after preparing bottles or serving food, before and after diapering or toileting, before and after first aid, before and after giving medication, before working with children at the beginning of the day, before leaving the classroom for a break or at the end of the day, and after wiping a nose, blowing a nose, coughing, or sneezing (see Figure 4–5).

Install soap and disposable paper towels near the sink; they are an integral part of hand washing. Turn on the warm water and adjust it to achieve a comfortable temperature. Wet hands and apply soap. Wash hands vigorously for approximately 15–20 seconds. The soap, along with the scrubbing action, dislodges germs. Dry hands with a paper towel. If taps do not shut off automatically, turn taps off with a paper towel. Using a towel helps avoid recontamination of clean hands. Dispose of the paper towel in a lidded trash receptacle with a plastic liner. A trash can operated with a foot mechanism is an expensive option, but the hands-free action significantly reduces the possibility of recontaminating clean hands.

Install sinks with running hot (regulated by an antiscald device) and cold water, installed at the children's height to promote frequent use. Once infants or toddlers are able to move about the room, they become quite fascinated with water found at a sink or in a

Posted Hand Washing Procedures

1	Turn on warm water and adjust to comfortable temperature.	2	Wet hands and apply soap.	3	Wash vigorously for approximately 15–20 seconds.
4	Dry hands with paper towel.	5	Turn off faucet with paper towel.	6	Dispose of paper towel in a lidded trash receptacle with a plastic liner.

Use hand washing procedures for staff and children

- before and after preparing bottles or serving food.
- before and after diapering or toileting.
- before and after administering first aid.
- before and after giving medication.
- before working with the children and at the end of the day.
- before leaving the classroom for a break.
- after wiping nose discharge, coughing, or sneezing.
- before and after playing in the sand and water table.
- after playing with pets.
- after playing outdoors.

Reprinted with permission from the National Association of Child Care Professionals, http:www.naccp.org.

FIGURE 4–5 Posted Hand Washing Procedures

toilet. Install an off-and-on water valve at the teachers' height to prevent curious infants from "unscheduled water play," close bathroom doors when they are not in use, and do not leave buckets of water unattended to avoid a potential drowning.

EMPLOYING UNIVERSAL PRECAUTIONS AND THE PROPER USE OF GLOVES

In 1991 OSHA established a blood-borne pathogen standard mandating that measures to protect employees from exposure to potentially infected blood pathogens were necessary. Hepatitis B (HBV) and Human Immunodeficiency Virus (HIV) are the two most common blood-borne pathogens. HBV is a disease of the liver contracted by exposure to contaminated blood. It causes inflammation and destruction of the liver and if not cured can eventually lead to death. HIV is a virus that is contracted by contaminated body fluids and has the potential to lead to AIDS, which destroys the human immune system and can lead to death.

Center staff are commonly exposed to body fluids in the form of urine, feces, vomitus, sweat, saliva, breast milk, and nasal secretions. It is difficult to stress the importance of using universal precautions without sounding a fear alarm. Contracting a case of HIV/AIDS is highly unlikely; in fact, Kinnell reports "the Center for Disease Control and Prevention stated 'we have never documented a case of HIV being transmitted through biting'" (p. 48). Because it is impossible to know when a person is infected with such a disease all body fluids or secretions *must* be treated as if they are infected with disease.

In the event that exposure to another person's body fluids is necessary, put on a pair of disposable, moisture-proof gloves before making contact with the contaminated source.

To avoid delaying immediate intervention on behalf of the child, yet protect yourself from harmful exposure, place gloves in several convenient areas so they can be retrieved quickly. To avoid contaminating yourself with soiled gloves, take care to remove them properly. Instructions for proper gloving procedures are located in Appendix B. Post this next to the first aid directives for a quick reference. Follow your company's policies for disposal of contaminated supplies and equipment.

CLEANSING TOYS AND EQUIPMENT

Disinfect toilet seats, diapering areas, and water fountains with 10 percent bleach solution (one part chlorine bleach/nine parts water) or any registered EPA disinfectant prepared according to instructions. Registered EPA approval appears on the product label. Because you are providing care for several infants at once, it is important to maintain proper sanitation of the toys and the equipment you use each day. After an infant is finished with a toy or set of toys place it in a bucket or basket that is marked for soiled toys only (see Figure 4–6). When time permits, cleanse the toys with a cleaning solution such as a bleach solution of 50 parts per million (approximately ½ teaspoon of chlorine bleach to 1 gallon of water). Allow the toys to dry completely before they are used again. Use this same preparation to sanitize high chairs, infant seats, cribs, and bouncers between uses by different babies.

CLEANSING REFRIGERATORS AND FOOD PREP AREAS

In order to maintain a healthy, safe food preparation and storage area, you will need to keep the area clean and sanitized. Use a cleaning solution of 200 parts per million (approximately 1 tablespoon of chlorine bleach to 1 gallon of water) to wipe all surfaces in the food preparation area at least once a day. Wipe the food and formula refrigerator on a weekly basis with the same strength cleaning solution.

FIGURE 4–6 Make Sure to Label Soiled Toys Container

CLEANSING AND STERILIZING BOTTLES

After a baby has finished drinking a bottle of formula, disassemble the bottle immediately. Remove the liner and any labels and discard them. Remove the nipple from the collar and place them with the bottle in a designated container to be properly cleansed and sterilized. Clean and sterilize the bottles and all components before using them again (see Figure 4–7).

SAFE HANDLING OF FRESH BREAST MILK

Breast milk is an excellent source of nutrition for infants. In order to provide a safe food for the breast-fed infant, follow the outlined procedure to transport, store, and prepare breast milk.

1. Instruct the mother to pump and store milk either in a sterilized bottle or disposable nurser bag. Provide only enough milk for one feeding. Label the milk with the baby's name and the date and time it was collected.
2. Transport the expressed milk in an insulated container that maintains the milk at 41°F.
3. When milk is needed, choose the one with the oldest date first.
4. Use fresh, refrigerated breast milk within 48 hours of the time it was expressed.
5. Warm milk by holding the bag or bottle under warm running water or by placing it in a bowl of warm water for 5 minutes. A slow-cook crock pot can provide warm water continuously all day. Gently shake the milk before feeding in case any separation has occurred.

Procedure for Cleansing and Sterilizing Bottles, Nipples, Collars, and Caps

1. Prewash in hot water with detergent. Scrub the bottles and nipples inside and out with a bottle and nipple brush if necessary. Squeeze water through the nipple hole during the washing procedure.
2. Rinse well with clean hot water.
3. Completely immerse in a bleach solution of 50 parts per million (check with a chlorine strip). Use approximately ½ teaspoon of chlorine bleach to 1 gallon of water in the final rinse.
4. Bring a large pan of water to a boil, and add one teaspoon of white vinegar to avoid a chalky white buildup. Boil the nipples, collars, and caps for 3 minutes. If bottle liners are not used for the formula, then boil the clean bottles for 5 minutes to sterilize them.
5. Pour the sterilized pieces in a strainer.
6. Air dry thoroughly.
7. Your hands need to be clean and you need to take care in handling techniques to prevent contamination of the clean bottles and nipples.
8. Store the completely dried bottle equipment in a clean, covered, and labeled container away from food items.

FIGURE 4–7 Cleansing and Sterilizing Bottles, Nipples, Collars and Caps

6. Do not use the microwave; high heat will destroy some nutrients and create hot spots. Hot spots can cause dangerous scalding and mouth burns. The use of microwave ovens to warm baby food, formula, or breast milk is considered a poor practice in the early care and education community.

7. Test warmed milk with a National Safety Standard (NSF) approved kitchen food thermometer. Serve the milk at a tepid temperature, 72–80°F. Testing the milk with a drop on the wrist is no longer an acceptable practice. Treat human breast milk with the same precautions used when handling human blood.

8. Once a bottle is fed to the baby, discard any remainder. It is not advisable to return it to the refrigerator.

9. Many states require the teacher to wear gloves when feeding infants breast milk.

CHECK   Yes _____   No _____   if this is your state requirement.

SAFE HANDLING OF FROZEN BREAST MILK

1. Instruct the mother to pump and store milk either in a sterilized bottle or disposable nurser bag. Provide only enough milk for one feeding. Label the milk with the baby's name and the date and time it was collected. Leave enough room in the bag or bottle for expansion during freezing.

2. Transport the expressed milk in an insulated container that maintains the milk at 41°F or below.

3. When milk is needed, choose the one with the oldest date first.

4. If storing breast milk in a refrigerator freezer, discard it after 2 months. Frozen milk stored at 0°F in a deep freezer should be discarded after 6 months.

5. a. Warm milk by holding the bag or bottle under warm running water or by placing it in a bowl of warm water for 5 minutes. A slow-cook crock pot can provide warm water continuously all day. The milk will have separated so shake it gently while thawing or prior to the feeding.

   b. Another method of thawing is known as a "cold thaw." Place the breast milk in the refrigerator at 41°F or below. Label the bottle or bag with the time and date it was moved from the freezer to the refrigerator. Use it within 24 hours. Warm the milk just prior to feeding. Check your local licensing regulators to ascertain if this is an acceptable practice in your area.

6. Do not use the microwave; high heat will destroy some nutrients and create hot spots. Hot spots can cause dangerous scalding and mouth burns. The use of microwave ovens to warm baby food, formula, or breast milk is considered a poor practice in the early care and education community.

7. Once the milk is thawed using a "warm thaw method," use it within 1 hour or refrigerate the thawed milk for up to 3 hours. Discard milk after the times indicated if it is not used.

8. Test warmed milk with an NSF approved kitchen food thermometer. Serve the milk at a tepid temperature, 72–80°F. Testing the milk with a drop on the wrist is no longer an acceptable practice. Treat human breast milk with the same precautions used when handling human blood.

9. Many states require the teacher to wear gloves when feeding infants breast milk.

CHECK   Yes _____   No _____   if this is your state requirement.

REFERENCES

American Academy of Pediatrics, American Public Health Association, National Resource Center for Health and Safety in Child Care (2002). *Stepping Stones to Using Caring for Our Children* (2nd ed.). Elk Grove, IL: American Academy of Pediatrics.

Kinnell, G. (2002). *No biting.* St. Paul, MN: Redleaf Press.

Wong, D. (1999). *Whaley & Wong's care of infants and children* (6th ed.). St. Louis, MO: Mosby.

RECOMMENDED RESOURCES

California Department of Education (1995). *Keeping kids healthy: Preventing and managing communicable disease in child care.* Sacramento, CA, Author.

Church, D. S. (2004). *The MELALEUCA wellness guide* (8th ed.). Centenial, CO: RM Barry Publications.

Donowitz, L. G. (2001). *Infection control in the child care center and preschool* (5th ed.). Hagerstown: Lippincott Williams & Wilkins.

CHAPTER

5

Health

To find your specific
State's Licensing, Rules
and Regulations go to:

http://nrc.uchsc.edu

SICK BAY AND ISOLATION AREA

Centers need to prepare a sick bay and an isolation area for a sick child to rest until a parent or guardian can call for him or her. Equip a space or room (depending on state regulations) with a crib in an area where an infant can be supervised constantly. Select a variety of toys and books to offer the little one until his or her departure. Provide a thermometer to measure body temperature and a container large enough to catch emesis in case the child vomits. Place a child-size chair in the area for a child to sit in while you administer first aid. For convenience, locate a locked medication/first aid cabinet and a small refrigerator nearby stocked with a lidded container labeled "refrigerated medications only," ice in baggies or cold packs, popsicles (for mouth and lip injuries), juice boxes, and fresh drinking water.

FIRST AID CABINET AND FIRST AID KITS

Minor injuries are common in a center setting. Children will experience scratches and bumps as they go about their daily activities. Prepare a first aid cabinet and kits to use in the event of an accident. As previously mentioned, it is convenient to provide a first aid cabinet near the area used to isolate sick children. The first aid cabinet must remain locked at all times so it is not accessible to the children but is accessible to the staff at a moment's notice. If your center transports children, then provide a complete first aid kit in the vehicle. Stock the first aid cabinet with disposable nonporous gloves and an American Red Cross first aid manual, an American Academy of Pediatrics (AAP) standard first aid chart, or an equivalent first aid guide. Other items to include are a nonglass thermometer, bandages, Band-Aids, sterile gauze pads, a triangular cloth splint, a plastic splint for immobilizing a limb, scissors, tweezers, safety pins, adhesive strips, a disposable apron, protective glasses, and a pocket mouth-to-mouth resuscitation mask to open an airway.

Causing vomiting when a caustic or corrosive substance has been swallowed can cause further physical damage; for this reason best practices no longer recommends syrup of ipecac in child care facilities. Provide a source of running water and soap near the first aid station to cleanse wounds. If running water is not available on a field trip, use a waterless antiseptic hand cleaner. All items contaminated with blood should be placed in plastic bags. These materials must be handled according to your center policy.

First aid supplies should also be conveniently available on the playground. Some centers find it convenient to hang a fanny pack in each classroom near the door so the teacher can wear it on the playground or use it in the classroom for minor injuries. Because accidents on the playground often involve blood, the teacher will need to employ universal precautions before handling the child. If a fanny pack is not used, another option on the playground involves installing a mailbox on a post. Stock the mailbox with items such as disposable nonporous gloves, tissues, wipes, plastic trash bags, sterile gauze pads, and bandages. The mailbox will keep the items dry until they are needed.

ADMINISTERING AND MANAGING MEDICATIONS

Administering medications requires special attention to detail. In some states all personnel distributing medication must take a special class and earn a certification. Check your local regulations. Instruct all personnel to always wash their hands before administering medication and to make sure they always match the name of the child with the label on the medication. Double check the proper dose. Always use a medication spoon or measuring spoon to be certain the proper dosage is administered. Follow the instructions for how frequently the medication should be given and whether it should be given before or after eating. Once the medication is given, document it on the Daily Medication sheet shown in Figure 5–1. The directions for using the Daily Medication sheet are explained further in this chapter.

Medications prescribed for an individual baby must be kept in the original container bearing the original pharmacy label showing the prescription number, the date it was filled, the physician's name, directions for use, and the child's name. When the medication is no longer needed, return it to the family. For the protection of the baby and yourself, do not give any over-the-counter medications without prior written approval from the infant's physician and the parents. Occasionally, an infant will develop symptoms of illness such as a high fever, persistent cough, or ear pain caused by infection. Sometimes there is a lapse in time before the parents/guardians can arrive to attend to their ill baby. It takes time to locate working parents, especially if they are not in the office or if they must wait for a replacement before leaving work (e.g., nurses or firefighters). Have presigned, approved physician orders on hand for fever-reducing medications and such in the event medication is needed promptly. With the orders in place, an authorized person can approve the use of medication over the phone. Provide the parents and their physician with a specific medication record. Include the date, the baby's name, the type of medication, how much medication is to be administered, and how often the dosage should be repeated (see Figure 5–1 on page 52). Make sure this copies with your state regulations. Sign the Daily Medication record with your full name and the time the medication is administered to maintain an accurate medication history (see Figure 5–2). Store all medications requiring refrigeration in a container with a lid marked *refrigerated medication*. Store any medications that do not require refrigeration in a locked cabinet that is inaccessible to the children (see Figure 5–3 on page 53).

Place the Daily Medication record near the Infant Receiving sheet to make it easy for the parents/guardian to record daily medication instructions.

ALLERGIES AND POSTING ALLERGY NOTICES

Allergies are caused by a variety of culprits know as allergens. Some can be triggered by a range of substances that include: venom, nuts, latex, certain drugs, stings, pollen, dust, mold, animal dander, and shellfish. A severe reaction can occur quickly, usually within a few minutes. Severe reactions are usually dramatic, with symptoms such as swelling of the face; tight, difficult breathing; or hives that look like red blotches on the skin. Mild allergic reactions are more common than severe ones. Milder allergic reactions display the same symptoms in much weaker forms and take longer to develop. Local reactions such as swelling of an entire arm or leg can be severe but are not commonly lethal. If a child has a severe allergy, recommend that the child wear a Medic Alert bracelet for immediate identification of the allergen if an exposure ever occurs. Severe reactions can

Medical Authorization
For Nonprescription Medication*

Name of Child: _____Jessie (Enter Last Name)_____   Date: _____09-18-2009_____

The staff is authorized to dispense the following medications as ordered by your physician and directed by the parents/guardian.

Please indicate specific medication, route it is given, dosage, and frequency.

Type	Medication	Route	Dosage	Frequency
Nonaspirin Preparation	Tylenol	By mouth	.4 cc	Every 4 hours over 101° as needed Send Home
Aspirin Preparation				
Cough Preparation	Robitussin	By mouth	1/2 tsp	Every 6 hours for persistent cough
Decongestant				
Skin Ointment	Desitin	On perineum	Thin layer	Every diaper change when redness develops
Diaper Wipes	Any brand	As directed		As needed
Sunscreen	Any brand	On skin	Small amount	Before outdoor play

_____Dr. Randall_____   _____Dr. Randall_____   _____XXX-XXX-XXXX_____
Print Name of Physician   Signature of Physician   Phone Number

_____Mr. Howard_____
Parent / Guardian Signature

Complete this form on admission and update annually. Store medical authorizations in an index box and place in or near locked cabinet for quick referencing.

FIGURE 5–1 Medical Authorization for Nonprescription Medication Sample

Daily Medication Sheet

Child's Name	RX Number & Type of Medication	Amount & Route Administered	Date	Time	Given by: First Name	Last Name
Carmela	RX 652201 Amoxicillin 250 Milligrams	1 tsp by mouth	02-22	11:00 am	Mr.	Hoffriah
				5:00 pm	Ms.	Salay

FIGURE 5–2 Daily Medication Sheet Sample

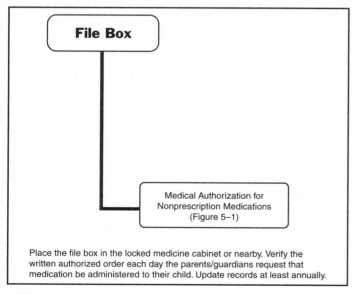

FIGURE 5–3 File Box for Record Keeping

be life threatening. Anaphylactic shock will very quickly interfere with the child's ability to breathe. If a child in attendance at the center has a known anaphylactic shock history, then a kit for epinephrine injections should remain on the premises and all staff should be familiar with how to administer it. Call 9-1-1 or the appropriate number if the infant is exposed to a known allergen or begins to exhibit signs of a severe reaction. Milder reactions, although not life threatening, will need a doctor's care, especially if the reaction has not occurred before.

On the KIDEX for Infants Individual Monthly Profile and Introduce Us to Your Baby, a space is provided for listing and recording any allergies an infant might have. Always post a list of all allergies in the KIDEX Class Book.

PREPARING FORMULA IN BOTTLES

If breast milk is not available for feeding, choose unopened commercially premixed formula or ready-to-feed formula as another optimum source for feeding. Since it is already mixed there is no chance of mixing errors; the baby is sure to receive the proper nutrition. Once a can of formula is opened, use it within 24 hours; after that, it is no longer considered safe to use. Concentrated formula and powdered formula are acceptable and more economically feasible but require mixing. Proper mixing is imperative to ensure the proper delivery of nutrition. Errors in mixing can deprive the infant of important nutrients or provide a formula that is too rich. Because of the potential for errors, some state licensing agencies prohibit the use of any formulas requiring mixing without written permission by the infant's physician indicating that a health condition requires it.

Prepare a day's supply of bottles at one time before the children arrive. Label each bottle with the child's name, the date, and the hour it was prepared. If the label is affixed to the plastic liner it is easily removed after use and does not leave sticky adhesive that is difficult to clean and sanitize. Pour the formula directly into a sanitized bottle or into a sanitized nurser hull with a sterile disposable liner, and affix a sanitized nipple. Store the prepared bottles in a refrigerator at 41°F.

SAFE HANDLING OF JARRED FOODS

Although commercially prepared jarred foods will retain their nutrient values for up to three to four days when properly refrigerated, most state licensing regulators require them to be used within 24 hours, after which they must be discarded. Once a jar is opened, dish out the portion needed into a feeding container, cover the jar, date it, and refrigerate it. Place in a dish only the amount needed for that particular feeding. Avoid serving the food directly from the jar, or it will become contaminated with baby's saliva. If an infant is fed directly from the jar, then discard the remaining portion following the feeding. To ensure food is not contaminated, accept only unopened jars for use in the infant room.

Warm baby's food in a pot of hot water. Be very careful to stir the food and test it to prevent hot spots from burning a baby's sensitive mouth or tongue. For safety, serve foods heated between 90 and 120°F.

MEASURING BODY TEMPERATURE

If you suspect a baby is overly warm or has an elevated temperature, measure and record his or her body temperature. The safest way to record an infant's temperature is under the arm, also known as an auxiliary temperature. The average normal auxiliary temperature is 97.4°F or 36.3°C. If you are using an electronic thermometer, then hold it in place until you hear a beeping sound. Report any elevated body temperatures immediately. Initiate an illness report and notify the attending supervisor so the parents/guardians can be contacted. Medicate the child if instructed by the parents/guardians or physician. Record the baby's temperature reading on the daily chart. Continue checking the baby's temperature every 30 minutes to monitor any drastic changes until the family arrives.

INDIVIDUAL ILLNESS AND TRACKING REPORTS

Begin each day with a general health assessment of each baby. Familiarity with each infant will help detect any unusual physical symptoms. If an infant you care for has a preexisting medical condition or a physical disability, become familiar with his or her particular needs. Minor illnesses are often reflected in the baby's general appearance: glassy eyes, flushed cheeks, swollen glands, or sluggish behavior. Isolate sick children from the group if they have a temperature that exceeds 100°F, symptoms of vomiting (one to three forceful rushes), diarrhea (defined as watery, mucous, foul-smelling bowel movement), or an undiagnosed rash. If you suspect a baby is exhibiting any of these symptoms, then complete an illness report with details and give it to the director/lead teacher to initiate the next step. Once the director/lead teacher determines the baby is sick, the parents should be notified.

Parents often feel frustration and guilt coupled with anxiety about having a sick baby and missing work. Be certain the baby is ill before disturbing the parents. If at any time a baby is exposed to a communicable illness such as chicken pox, measles, and so forth, post a notice on the Infant Current Events Bulletin Board. Descriptions of common communicable illnesses and symptoms can be found in Chapter 8. It is helpful to give the parents a copy of the illness report so they will have details in hand about the symptoms to take with them to the physician (see Figure 5–4). Track reports of illnesses on a daily basis to identify epidemic patterns in the center (see Figure 5–5).

HEAD LICE

Whenever children are cared for in groups, head lice infestation is possible. Children with head lice infestation usually have older siblings who attend elementary school and unsuspectingly carry it home to their family. Head lice are a potential problem but do not indicate a family is dirty: it can happen to anyone. Head lice can be picked up anywhere, including movie theaters, a bus, or an airline seat. In a child care setting infestation is more likely to occur if clothing is stored so that infested clothing touches others.

To reduce the possibility of a head lice epidemic in your center, the program will need to be proactive and employ weekly head checks for every child. Figure 5–6 is an example of a completed Head Lice Checklist. Take measures to ensure this information remains confidential.

SUGGESTED ILLNESS

Child's name: _____Courtney (Enter Last Name)_____   Date: _____10/04/xx_____

SYMPTOMS ARE:

_____102°_____   Body Temperature (under arm, add 1 degree)

_____   Vomiting

_____   Diarrhea

_____   Exhibiting signs of a communicable illness

_____   Skin condition requiring further treatment

Other: _____Complaining her left ear hurts_____

Report initiated by: _____Mr. Eagle_____

Were parents notified? Yes __✔__ No _____ By whom? _Mrs. Gilreath_

Time parents notified: 1st Attempt _1:30 pm_   _____Dad_____
                                                      Which Parent Notified
                           2nd Attempt _1:35 pm_   _____Mom_____
                                                      Which Parent Notified
                           3rd Attempt _____   _____
                                                      Which Parent Notified

Time child departed: _____1:50 pm_____

Director's signature: _____Ms. Niehoff_____

Children exhibiting a temperature that exceeds 100°F, symptoms of vomiting (1–3 forceful rushes), diarrhea (defined as watery, mucous, foul-smelling bowel movement) or an unrecognized rash shall not return to group care for a minimum of 24 hours after treatment or before symptoms subside.

1. Office Copy   2. Parent/Guardian Copy

FIGURE 5–4 Suggested Illness Sample

Illness Tracking Reports

Name of Child	Date	Time Called	Type of Illness	Person Reporting Illness	Director Notified	Report Filed	Parent Notified	Time Left
Emily (Enter Last Name)	1/26	12:30 pm	Fever 101°	Mrs. Willis				1:30 pm
Jaden (Enter Last Name)	1/27	11:00 am	Diarrhea	Ms. Sutton				11:15 am
Olivia (Enter Last Name)	1/27	2:00 pm	Vomiting	Mr. Thurmond				2:30 pm
Marta (Enter Last Name)	1/28	7:30 am	Earache	Mrs. Hiland				8:00 am
Chen (Enter Last Name)	1/29	8:15 am	Headache	Ms. Day				8:45 am
Joshua (Enter Last Name)	1/30	4:00 pm	Split Lip	Mr. Law				4:30 pm
Andrew (Enter Last Name)	1/30	4:30 pm	Fever 100°	Mrs. Lane				4:45 pm

FIGURE 5–5 Illness Tracking Reports Sample

Head Lice Checklist

Group Name: ___The Peaches___

Name	Sunday	Monday	Tuesday	Wednesday	Thursday	Friday	Saturday
Bailey		A	C	C	A	A	
Emily		C	C	C	C	C	
Jared		C	C	C	C	C	
Jenni		C	C	A	C	C	
Mary		C	C	C	C	C	
Robert		C	C	C	C	C	
Kellie		C	A	C	C	C	
Erin		C	C	C	C	C	
Jan		C	C	C	C	C	
Tamika		C	C	C	A	C	
Natosha		C	C	C	C	C	
Mitch		C	C	C	C	C	
Harry		C	C	C	C	C	

C = Clear   **A = Absent**   **P = Possible**

(**Reminder**: *Please check weekly on different days of the week.*)

FIGURE 5–6 Head Lice Checklist

REFERENCES

Hentges, D. (May 1966). Keeping food safe for baby. National Network for Child Care's (NNCC). *Connections Newsletter,* 1–2. Retrieved from http://www.nncc.org

RECOMMENDED RESOURCES

Aronson, S. S., & Shope, T. R. *Managing infectious diseases in child care and schools.* Elk Grove, IL: American Academy of Pediatrics.

Kemper, K. J. (1996). *The holistic pediatrician.* New York: HarperCollins.

HELPFUL WEB SITES

Health and Safety Tips, *Immunizations.* http://www.nrc.vchsc.edu

Health and Safety Tips, *Medication administration in the child care setting.* http://www.nrc.vchsc.edu

Health and Safety Tips, *Daily health checks.* http://www.nrc.uchsc.edu

Safety

To find your specific
State's Licensing, Rules
and Regulations go to:

http://nrc.uchsc.edu

To ensure the safety and well-being of all people in the child care setting it is necessary to create policies that promote safety practices and prepare for potential emergencies. Establishing policies and procedures in advance and implementing drills to practice the outlined procedures will build staff confidence and reduce ensuing chaos should an emergency occur.

INDIVIDUAL ACCIDENT/INCIDENT REPORTS AND TRACKING OCCURRENCES

If a baby is injured during the course of the day, complete an Accident/Incident Report (see Figure 6–1). The Accident/Incident Report will describe the type of injury, its location on the body, and what time it occurred. It will also answer the following questions: Was blood present? If so, were universal precautions employed? What type of treatment was rendered and who witnessed the accident? After this report is completed, send it to the director/lead teacher for review. Contact the family and inform them of the injuries so they can decide, with the center personnel, if they desire further treatment for their baby. Some parents are more likely to seek medical treatment than others, and it is a decision they are entitled to make. Some states require the center to submit a copy of the Accident/Incident Report to its licensing consultant if the injury required medical intervention by a doctor, clinic, or hospital. This form is a legal document so great care must be exercised to complete it accurately. Describe the injury rather than assign a diagnosis. For example, describe an injury as a purple mark the size of a dime on the right cheek rather than a bruise or contusion on the face. If you are unsure of how to describe an injury accurately, it is best to obtain assistance from a supervisor.

In child care centers it is helpful to track accident/incident and illness trends. Create a binder specifically to collect and record all Accident/Incident and Illness Reports. On a daily basis, log Accident/Incident Tracking Reports (Figure 6–2 on page 60) and Illness Tracking Reports (see Figure 5–5). This requires a few moments daily. The director/lead teacher can use it as a handy reference to track possible illness trends such as influenza or RSV, or perhaps discover a pattern of accidents/incidents that are occurring in a specific group, such as biting or falls. If your center maintains a copy of individual accident/incident and illness reports, store them in the binder with the tracking reports (see Figure 6–3 on page 60). If they are stored in each child's individual file, they are considered, by law, a part of the child's permanent record.

POSTING FIRST AID DIRECTIVES

Early care and education professionals who are adequately trained in cardiopulmonary resuscitation (CPR), artificial respiration, and first aid procedures are an asset to the

Accident/Incident

Child's Name: _____Agnes (Enter Last Name)_____

Date of accident/injury: _____04/30/xx_____ Time: _____3:00 pm_____

Brief description of accident/injury: _____Agnes was crawling after a_____

ball and collided with Herald. She received a cut on her arm about the size

of a nickel.

Was first aid given? _____Yes_____ If so, describe: _Washed her arm with soap_

_& water. Applied bandage to arm.._____

Was blood present in accident? ___Yes___ How much? _____Small amount_____

Were Universal Precautions employed? _____Yes_____

Was medical intervention required?* _____No_____ If yes, describe: _____

_____

Person initiating this report: __Ms. Harrison__ Witness: ____Ms. Lawson____

Name of parent contacted: ___Ms. Sutton___ Time contacted: ____3:15 pm____

Director's signature: _____Mrs. Wright_____

*In some states it is required to file a copy of this report with the child care licensing department if medical intervention is required.

FIGURE 6–1 Accident/Incident Report

Accident/Incident Tracking Reports

Name of Child	Date	Time Called	Type of Accident	Person Reporting Accident	Director Notified	Report Filed	Parent Notified	Time Left
David (Enter Last Name)	1/26	10:30 am	Fell & hurt right elbow	Mrs. Runisfeld	✓	✓	✓	11:00 am
Agnes (Enter Last Name)	1/27	3:15 pm	Tripped & fell down, she scraped her left elbow & right knee	Mr. Meda	✓	✓	✓	3:30 pm

FIGURE 6–2 Accident/Incident Tracking Reports

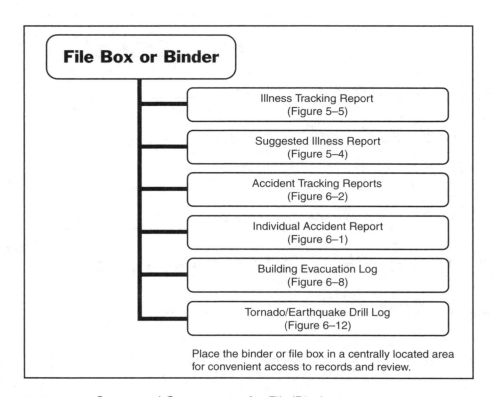

FIGURE 6–3 Suggested Components for File/Binder

children they care for. It is advisable for all child care personnel to receive and maintain current CPR, artificial respiration, and first aid training.

Post first aid directives in each room to serve as a quick reminder of what steps to follow in case of an emergency. First aid directives are a brief review of what to do if an emergency does occur. There are many different kinds of emergencies. In Figure 6–4 some of the most common emergencies are listed, such as: poisoning, bleeding, choking, seizures, shock, and situations requiring artificial respiration. Place the directives next to each phone along with the phone numbers for the poison control center, the fire department, emergency help, medical, dental, ambulance, and the police station. When pertinent information is readily available in an emergency situation, it can help staff remain calm enough to perform at an optimum level.

ESTABLISHING FIRE DRILLS AND EMERGENCY EVACUATION

Emergency procedures need to be in place and well practiced long before the occurrence of an urgent situation. Advance preparation and practice on a regular basis are necessary to teach the staff and children how to react in a calm manner when an emergency does occur. Preparing for potential emergencies involves a variety of deliberately planned actions. The region you live in will determine the types of emergencies the center might encounter, such as hurricanes, tornadoes, or earthquakes. The potential always exists for physical accidents or sudden illness requiring advanced medical intervention. Emergencies such as fires, bomb threats, or gas leaks are all situations that require immediate evacuation of the building to safeguard its occupants.

A complete emergency plan includes posting emergency phone numbers and evacuation plans in every occupied room of the building. Place by every phone a list of emergency contacts for quick reference (see Figure 6–5 on page 63). Conduct emergency drills at least monthly. Every room in which babies are cared for requires a very specific outline of instructions and procedures that are to be followed in case of an emergency. Post this in a visible location. The instructions need to include what exit to use in a situation requiring the infants to be removed from the building (see Figure 6–6 on page 64). When it is necessary to remove the infants from the building, place the babies in a sturdy bed that has been prepared with heavy wheel casters, and follow the specific instructions outlined for the emergency exit procedure.

Familiarize yourself with this information long before a drill occurs. It is helpful to have a large blanket available and an emergency bag in case re-entry into the building is delayed. Figure 6–7 (see page 65) lists how to assemble an emergency bag. Replenish and maintain the emergency bag at all times so it is available at a moment's notice. The director/lead teacher will keep a record of what day and time emergency drills take place, as well as how long it takes for the center to completely evacuate all the children *safely* (see Figures 6–8, 6–9, 6–10, 6–11, and 6–12 on pages 65–68).

SAFE SLEEPING POSITIONS

In order to reduce the possibility of Sudden Infant Death Syndrome, it is no longer advisable to lay an infant on its stomach or face down during sleep. If an infant is unable to move its body from side to side or front to back, then always place him or her on his or her side with a rolled blanket or towel to support his or her back while sleeping. This position will help prevent the dangerous aspiration of any stomach contents that might be regurgitated. Once the infant is able to move from side to side and front to back, then place him or her on his or her back for sleeping. An article describing Sudden Infant Death Syndrome is located in Chapter 8.

SUGGESTED FIRST AID DIRECTIVES

CHOKING

(Conscious) - Stand or kneel behind child with your arms around his waist and make a fist. Place thumb side of fist in the middle of abdomen just above the navel. With moderate pressure, use your other hand to press fist into child's abdomen with a quick, upward thrust. Keep your elbows out and away from child. Repeat thrusts until obstruction is cleared or child begins to cough or becomes unconscious.

(Unconscious) - Position child on his back. Just above navel, place heel of one hand on the midline of abdomen with the other hand placed on top of the first. Using moderate pressure, press into abdomen with a quick, upward thrust. Open airway by tilting head back and lifting chin. **If you can see the object**, do a finger sweep. Slide finger down inside of cheek to base of tongue, sweep object out but be careful not to push the object deeper into the throat. Repeat above until obstruction is removed or child begins coughing. If child does not resume breathing, proceed with artificial respiration (see below).

Infants - Support infant's head and neck. Turn infant face down on your forearm. Lower your forearm onto your thigh. Give four (4) back blows forcefully between infant's shoulder blades with heel of hand. Turn infant onto back. Place middle and index fingers on breastbone between nipple line and end of breastbone. Quickly compress breastbone one-half to one inch with each thrust. Repeat backblows and chest thrusts until object is coughed up, infant starts to cry, cough, and breathe, or medical personnel arrives and takes over.

POISONING

Call Poison Control Center (1-800-382-9097) immediately! Have the poison container handy for reference when talking to the center. Do not induce vomiting unless instructed to do so by a health professional. Check the child's airway, breathing, and circulation.

HEMORRHAGING

Use a protective barrier between you and the child (gloves). Then, with a clean pad, apply firm continuous pressure to the bleeding site for five minutes. Do not move/change pads, but you may place additional pads on top of the original one. If bleeding persists, call the doctor or ambulance Open wounds may require a tetanus shot.

SEIZURE

Clear the area around the child of hard or sharp objects. Loosen tight clothing around the neck. Do not restrain the child. Do not force fingers or objects into the child's mouth. After the seizure is over and if the child is not experiencing breathing difficulties, lay him/her on his/her side until he/she regains consciousness or until he/she can be seen by emergency medical personnel. After the seizure, allow the child to rest. Notify parents immediately. If child is experiencing breathing difficulty, or if seizure is lasting longer than 15 minutes, call an ambulance at once.

ARTIFICIAL RESPIRATION *(Rescue Breathing)*

Position child on the back; if not breathing, open airway by gently tilting the head back and lifting chin. Look, listen, and feel for breathing. If still not breathing, keep head tilted back and pinch nose shut. Give two full breaths and then one regular breath every 4 seconds thereafter. Continue for one minute; then look, listen, and feel for the return of breathing. Continue rescue breathing until medical help arrives or breathing resumes.

If using one-way pulmonary resuscitation device, be sure your mouth and child's mouth are sealed around the device.

(Modification for infants only)   Proceed as above, but place your mouth over nose and mouth of the infant. Give light puffs every 3 seconds.

SHOCK

If skin is cold and clammy, as well as face pale or child has nausea or vomiting, or shallow breathing, call for emergency help. Keep the child lying down. Elevate the feet. If there are head/chest injuries, raise the head and shoulders only.

To find your specific
State's Licensing, Rules
and Regulations go to:

http://nrc.uchsc.edu

FIGURE 6-4 Suggested First Aid Directives

Emergency Contacts: *Post Near Every Telephone*

Your Facility Address: _____*(Enter Street #)*_____

_____*(Enter City, State, and Zip Code)*_____

Nearest Main Intersection: _____*92nd and Main Street*_____

Your Facility Phone Number: _____*xxx-xxx-xxxx*_____

Contact	Phone Number
Operator	*0*
Emergency	*911*
Fire	*xxx-xxx-xxxx*
Police	*xxx-xxx-xxxx*
Consulting Dentist	*xxx-xxx-xxxx*
Poison Control	*xxx-xxx-xxxx*
Local Hospital Emergency Dept	*xxx-xxx-xxxx*
Other	
Other	

FIGURE 6–5 Emergency Contacts example

LEAVING THE ROOM UNATTENDED

Child/adult ratios are established and maintained for classroom safety. A room with children present should *never* be left unattended by an adult! Leaving children unattended puts them in a potentially dangerous situation. Open your door and alert someone, or pick up the telephone (if it's nearby) and page for help. When it becomes necessary to leave your room, arrange for another adult to cover for you.

Emergency Exit Evacuation

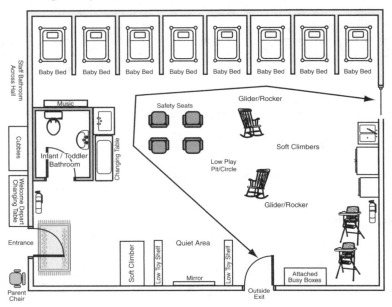

Equip 1-2 infant cribs depending on the crib size and how many children you are caring for in your group. For example equip at least two junior size cribs for eight infants. Mark the beds for emergency use and place them in a close proximity to the designated exit. Draw two exit routes on the emergency evacuation plan template provided. List who to call in case of fire, bomb threat, gas leak, etc. Draw on template where fire extinguisher is located.

Center's Address: _____*(Enter Street #)*_____

Nearest Main Intersection: _____*(Enter Street #)*_____

Center's Phone Number: _____*xxx-xxx-xxxx*_____

In Case of Fire Call: _____*xxx-xxx-xxxx*_____

In Case of Bomb Threat Call: _____*xxx-xxx-xxxx*_____

In Case of Gas Leak Call: _____*xxx-xxx-xxxx*_____

Fire Extinguisher expires Date: _____*11-05-2009*_____

Emergency Bag and Blanket are located: _____*in closet of main hallway*_____

Place infants in the emergency evacuation beds. If the door is cool, open door slowly, make sure fire or smoke isn't blocking your escape route. If your escape is blocked close the door and use alternative escape route. Smoke and heat rise be prepared to crawl where the air is clearer and cooler near the floor. Move as far from the building as possible. In case of real fire do not reenter the building until it is cleared by the proper authorities.

Figure 6–6 Emergency Exit Evacuation example

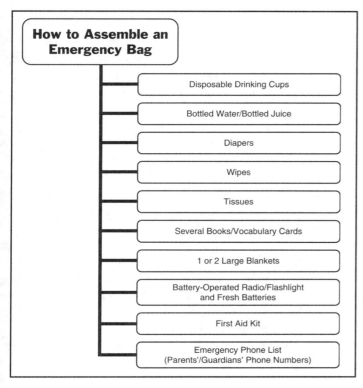

FIGURE 6–7 Emergency Bag Components

Building Evacuation Log

Date	Time of Drill	Evacuation Time	Comments	Full Name of Person in Charge
04-13	7:15 am	1 min 30 sec	Great Job!	Ms. Lopez
05-23	12:00 pm	1 min 45 sec		Ms. Lopez
06-15	2:45 pm	2 min 10 sec		Ms. Lopez
07-30	10:45 am	1 min 50 sec		Ms. Lopez

FIGURE 6–8 Building Evacuation Log

ACCIDENT PREVENTION

SAFE USA reports that in one year, approximately 7,000 children were sent to the hospital for falls from high chairs. Baby walker–related injuries resulted in more than 16,000 children receiving treatment in hospital emergency rooms. 80 percent of the accidents occurred while the babies were being supervised (July 2002).

Infants are extremely active. When a baby is on a changing table, best practices encourages keeping one hand on his or her body at all times. If your attention is required somewhere else, then put the baby on the floor or carry the baby with you if that is feasible.

Avoid using safety straps during diaper changes because of the high risk of cross-contamination with bacteria. In other instances safety straps are very useful. Most baby equipment such as high chairs, infant seats, bouncy chairs, or strollers is equipped with safety straps. The most effective straps include a waist strap and one that extends between the legs. The latter strap prevents the baby from slipping down in a seat and being strangled. The safety straps in your infant room will sustain heavy usage and eventually wear thin and require replacement long before the equipment has served its full life. The straps can be replaced by the original manufacturer or found from a source such as Custom Straps, http://www.ahh.biz or toll free 866-458-2559.

Some accidents are caused by a high chair tipping over. A high chair might tip if an active child pushes off from a table or wall, stands up in the high chair, or rocks back and forth. Pick high chairs that have wide bases (http://www.babyparenting.about.com).

Tornado Emergency Instructions

Your county or region is: _Marion County_

Tornado Watch: A tornado is possible. Remain alert for approaching storms. Tune your portable (battery-operated) radio to a local weather station.

Tornado Warning: A tornado has been sighted. Activate your emergency shelter plan immediately.

Grab your emergency bag and blanket. They are located: _in main hallway closet_

_____

Place the infants in the designated emergency evacuation cribs and move calmly and quickly to an interior room or hallway. Account for all children in attendance.
Your best location is: _main hallway past library_

_____

Cover cribs with a blanket in case of flying glass or debris. Avoid windows, doors, outside walls, and corners of rooms.

FIGURE 6–9 Tornado Emergency Instructions

Earthquake Emergency Instructions

Prior to earthquakes:
- Brace high and top-heavy objects.
- Fasten cubbies, lockers, toy shelves to the wall.
- Anchor overhead lighting fixtures.
- Install flexible pipe fitting to avoid gas or water leaks.
- Know when and how to shut off electricity, gas, and water at main switches and valves.
- Locate safe spots in the room to protect yourself from dropping debris such as under a sturdy table or crib.

Your safest location is: _in the hallway under library tables_

The shutoff for gas is located: _in the basement next to furnace_

The water main is located: _in the kitchen next to large sink_

Your emergency bag is located: _on top shelf of toy cabinet_

During an earthquake:

- Stay inside until shaking stops and it is safe to go outside.
- Move the infants to your safe location (inside a crib on an inside wall).
- Place a heavy blanket or lightweight mattress over the crib.
- If you are on the playground, move away from the building.

When the shaking stops be prepared for aftershocks. Check for injuries and administer first aid as indicated. Use flashlights if electricity is out. Do not light candles or matches in case of gas leakage.

FIGURE 6–10 Earthquake Emergency Instructions

Baby walkers are not considered safe. Baby walkers give children more mobility than they are ready for developmentally. Baby walkers make it easier for infants to reach dangerous things on tables—things they would not be able to reach if they were crawling (http://www.safeusa.org; search under "falls"). A safer choice is a stationary play station such as an Exersaucer, found in most baby supply and toy stores, online at http://www. ebabysuperstore.com or by calling 866-771-2229.

CRIB AND MATTRESS SAFETY

Promote sanitary sleeping conditions by placing baby cribs at least 3 feet apart unless they are separated by a wall from floor to ceiling. Assign each infant his or her own crib if possible.

Completely wash each crib on a weekly basis or in between uses by different infants. The crib will need to be completely sanitized with a cleaning solution such as a bleach

---

Hurricane Emergency Instructions

Hurricane/Tropical Storm Watch: indicates the conditions are possible in the specific area within 36 hours.

Hurricane/Tropical Storm Warning: conditions are expected within 24 hours.

Send the children home.
Learn your specific evacuation route.
Secure your facility.
Close storm shutters.
Turn utilities off at main valves if instructed by authorities.
Take emergency phone numbers with you.

Your Evacuation Route: _turn right on west 86th street, drive 2 blocks to_

Meridian, turn right, go 1/4 of a mile to Interstate 465 West for 2 miles, then Interstate

865 to Interstate 65 to North Carolina

Figure 6–11 Hurricane Emergency Instructions

Tornado / Earthquake Drill Log

Date	Time of Drill	Time Needed to Seek Cover	Comments	Full Name of Person in Charge
2/14	2:30 PM	2 minutes	Well Done!	Miss Ferdahard

Figure 6–12 Tornado/Earthquake Drill Log

solution of 100 parts per million, approximately 1 teaspoon to 1 gallon of water. Clean and wipe the bed rails on a regular basis to reduce the spread of bacteria.

Change all bed clothing immediately when wet or soiled and at least once a day. If your center changes infants in cribs then you will need to place a clean waterproof pad on the bedding before changing in order to protect the bedding, or a fresh sheet will need to be put on after each changing.

If the cribs you are using have adjustable mattress heights, lower the mattress on a regular basis as appropriate to match the growth of the baby. Many infant cribs have a bed rail that moves up and down. Avoid a head injury or dangerous fall by placing the crib rail up in a locked position whenever a baby is occupying the crib.

Choose sturdy cribs with bars that are not more than 2⅜ inches apart. Many companies offer heavy-duty portacrib-size beds. Portacribs help conserve space and are needed only for naps and possible diaper changes. A firm waterproof mattress is your best choice. The gap between the mattress and the crib should not exceed 1 inch to prevent possible suffocation.

Use the crib only for naps and possibly for diaper changes. The crib is not an appropriate place for extended play activities. Once a baby has awakened from his or her nap, remove him or her promptly to a more appropriate play area.

Crib mobiles and toys that string across a crib are stimulating for young infants, but once a baby is five to six months old and is more active, these types of toys can present a strangulation hazard. Permanently remove any mobiles and toys of this nature from the crib once a baby is able to sit up and reach for them.

SAFETY PLUG COVERS

For the safety of all the infants, check electrical outlets for safety plug covers on a daily basis. Standard 5.048, *Safety Covers and Shock Protection Devices for Electrical Outlets,* from *Caring for Our Children, National Health and Safety Performance Standards* (2nd ed.), encourages the use of safety plug covers that are attached to the electrical receptacle by a screw or other means to prevent easy removal by a child. Avoid using outlet covers that a child can pull from the socket. All newly installed electrical outlets accessible to children should be protected by ground-fault circuit-interrupter (GFCI) shock protection devices or safety receptacles that require simultaneous contact with both prongs of a plug to access the electricity. (American Academy of Pediatrics 2002). Several new safety plug outlets are now available for consumers. Babies are curious, and an unprotected electrical outlet is a potential for electrocution. If you are planning new construction, consider placing the electrical outlets at least 48 inches from the ground.

LATEX BALLOONS AND SMALL OBJECT HAZARDS

Latex balloons can be a very dangerous toy for infants and young children. Because they explore with their mouths, it is not uncommon for a baby or toddler to suck or bite a balloon, causing it to burst. Preschool children may attempt to inflate a balloon and run the risk of it deflating and blocking their airway. Best practices strongly discourage latex balloons, and they should not be permitted in a child care facility where young children are present. If the center shares playground space with school-age children, be very careful to clean up any latex pieces left by the older children. The same advice remains true for toy lending and swapping. For instance, if an older class borrows a set of the younger group's building blocks to help construct a "block city," double-check the returned items for any errant small objects such as marbles or puzzle pieces that could present a hazard for the younger group.

REFERENCES

American Academy of Pediatrics, American Public Health Association, National Resource Center for Health and Safety in Child Care. (2003) *Stepping Stones to Using Caring for Our Children* (2nd ed.), Elk Grove, IL: American Academy of Pediatrics.

High Chair Safety. Retrieved online 12/22/2004 from http://www.babyparenting.about.com.

SAFE USA. (July 14, 2002). Preventing childhood falls; Baby walkers. Retrieved online 12/22/2004 from http://safeusa.org/falls.html.

Facilitating Baby and Baby's Family

To find your specific State's Licensing, Rules and Regulations go to:

http://nrc.uchsc.edu

Routines are a big part of an infant's or toddler's day. Attending to, feeding, diapering, soothing, and cuddling babies; preparing them for sleep; coping with separation anxiety; creating a stimulating environment; and promoting safety and health are the most common elements of an infant teacher's day. Clark (2003) shares that "routines are great opportunities for learning experiences . . . and [teachers should] allow adequate time to accomplish them" (p. 77). Routines in an infant's day are an opportunity to engage in social interaction and create warm interpersonal relationships. Daily routines are enhanced with a great deal of smiling, talking, and touching. The child's family also benefits from established routines they can count on. For example, drop-off and pick-up times are busy times in the center. By creating organized routines to receive each infant and to facilitate departure, there will be less of an opportunity to miss important points necessary to provide quality care.

WELCOMING NEW PARENTS

New parents are considered "fragile clients." Separation from their new baby often produces a great deal of sadness and anxiety. For many parents this is the longest period of time they have been separated from their new infant. Often both parents need to maintain full-time employment for financial reasons, and they seek the very best care for their precious infant. After careful consideration, they choose a center that appears to be capable of rendering excellent care for their baby. This is a hand-holding stage. It is necessary for caregivers to go out of their way to establish a trusting relationship with a new baby and his or her family, especially those first couple of weeks (see Figure 7–1 for some tips).

Tips For The First Few Weeks

1. Invite one or both parents to visit the nursery the week before the baby starts attending to spend part of the day with the group to experience the nursery tempo.

2. Prepare a brown bag lunch for the mother during the first week. There is always so much to accomplish during that first week back to work that she will most likely put her needs last.

3. Arrange several check-in times a day during the first week to call so the mother doesn't feel she is pestering.

4. Take photos of the baby in action at the nursery. Frame one for her desk, and add a caption: "Mom, I'm making friends while you work."

5. Make a little spa pack with bath salts, a little candle, and a magazine for her to enjoy soon.

FIGURE 7–1 Parent/Caregiver Relationship Tips

Offer the families information about the daily routines. Welcome them into your group so they begin to feel comfortable and adapt to the schedule. As your relationship evolves, a level of trust develops and it becomes easier for them to move in and out when they drop off their little one. The child care personnel spend many hours in a given center. Once we become familiar with our routines it is easy to forget how it feels to be new to the center setting. Challenge yourself to look at each new family and recollect how you felt on your first day.

Clients are most fragile within the first several weeks of their stay at the center. It is imperative to establish trust and rapport quickly. Parents/guardians who feel left out of the loop sometimes assume their baby's needs are also not being met and might be inclined to make other child care arrangements. New parents appreciate an extra big welcome in the morning, and it is your role to include them in discussions while establishing care. Show them where to store the baby's personal belongings, where to sign in for the day, and where they can find the baby's daily sheets. Introduce them to other parents so they begin to feel a part of the group quickly.

Another time a client might be considered fragile is if an unusual situation occurs at the center such as frequent illnesses or erratic napping schedules that differ from the baby's home patterns. Trust becomes compromised when the parents begin to question whether the staff demonstrates concern for their individual challenges. Reassure the parents that you are very committed and sympathetic to their concerns. Share more information to assist their understanding. If a situation can be improved, outline what plan of action you have put into place to correct the situation or prevent it from recurring.

Parents naturally bond with the teachers through positive daily contact, but at times they may experience some dissatisfaction in other center matters. For example, they may experience an error with their billing or dislike how their billing has been handled. A mistake might be made that they do not feel comfortable discussing with the director or the office personnel. If you hear a parent voicing a concern, it is very helpful to share this observation with the director/lead teacher. It provides an opportunity to proactively alleviate any misunderstandings or clear up whatever frustrations the client may be experiencing. It takes a whole team to make child care a pleasant and positive experience for everyone, and it is very important to keep the lines of communication open on all levels. Managers, with their vast array of experience, will be able to smooth out matters quickly.

BABY'S ARRIVAL: RECEIVING BABY

Everyone appreciates a warm welcome upon arrival. Make an effort to greet your babies and their families as they arrive. At this age, maternal and paternal separation anxiety is at an all-time high. Your *warm* welcome will assist with a smooth separation and establish a deep level of comfort for the departing parent. Collecting pertinent information during morning arrival will provide a stable transition for the baby. Use the Infant Receiving Sheet to gather pertinent specific information from the parent regarding the baby's most recent activity such as the time the baby last awoke, when the baby last ate, when the last diaper change took place, and any comments they would like to make to assist with specific care that day (see Figure 7–2 for an example). The infant room is extra busy in the morning with arrivals. Place the Infant Receiving Sheet on a clipboard or writing surface in an easily accessible area so the parents can record information conveniently.

STAFF RATIOS AND TEACHER ASSIGNMENTS

Adequate staffing ratios not only support strong early care and teaching practices, but also reduce staff burnout and promote retention. Smaller group sizes provide the opportunity

Infant Receiving Sheet	Date:		_June 18th_	
Welcome, Baby!				
Infant's Name	**Time Baby Awoke**	**Last Feeding**	**Comments, if any**	**Last Diaper Change**
Carmela	5:45 am	7:30 am	Dr.'s Appt @ 2:15	7:30 am
Deepok	6:30 am	7:15 am		7:45 am
Jason	7:15 am	7:30 am	Rough night sleep	7:45 am
Marcus	6:45 am	7:00 am		7:30 am
Layla	7:00 am	7:30 am		7:45 am

Figure 7–2 Infant Receiving Sheet

for better supervision and consistent care. The infants benefit from smaller group interactions. Mistakes and missed procedures are far less likely to happen when adequate child/staff ratios are maintained.

Strive to limit the number of adults an infant interacts with during the course of care. Young infants thrive on security and consistency. Care is optimized when primary assignments are made. Assigning a primary teacher or consistent group of primary teachers to provide for each individual infant's needs will make the baby feel secure and ensure the many details necessary to promote excellent care are taken care of.

RECORDING DEVELOPMENTAL MILESTONES

It is very important to understand from the beginning that children will develop at similar rates but each in a unique pattern. All babies are individuals. They each have their own distinctive personalities so consequently they will each develop at a slightly different pace.

The following examples (Figures 7–3, 7–4, 7–5, and 7–6 on pages 73–76) provide a guide for observing and recording developmental milestones for each infant. Observe the infant's behaviors at each of the age ranges.

1. Check the behaviors with a *Y* for yes if the baby demonstrates this action regularly.
2. Mark *S* for sometimes if the baby is just beginning to demonstrate the action or only does it sometimes.
3. Mark *N* for not yet if the baby doesn't demonstrate this action yet. Use the listed developments as a guide for observing.

1-3 Months

DEVELOPMENTAL MILESTONES

BABY CAN:

Y   BEGIN TO SMILE AND WILL RESPOND TO SMILING

Y   LOOK AT HANDS

Y   BEGIN TO CONTROL HEAD MOVEMENTS

N   HOLD A RATTLE BRIEFLY

N   SQUEAL, COO, & LAUGH

Y   GLANCE FROM ONE THING TO ANOTHER

S   LIFT HEAD WHEN LYING ON STOMACH

N   ROLL FROM SIDE TO BACK

N   RAISE UP ON FOREARMS

Y   BRING OBJECTS TO MOUTH

N   SIT *SUPPORTED*

Y   TURN HEAD TOWARD VOICES OR SOUNDS

Y   EXPLORE OWN BODY PARTS *(ESP. HANDS & FEET)*

N   BEGIN TO REACH WITH ACCURACY

> *Important Note: Infants will develop at similar rates but each in a unique pattern. If you find a baby is not exhibiting the majority of characteristics listed, there could be many plausible reasons ranging from premature birth to a more reserved and cautious personality. This list is a broad overview and not inclusive of all developmental milestones baby will experience.*

BABY	*John*	CAREGIVER	*Ms. Feldman*	DATE	*5/9/xx*
Y = YES		S = SOMETIMES		N = NOT YET	

FIGURE 7-3 1-3 Months Developmental Milestones

4-6 Months

DEVELOPMENTAL MILESTONES

BABY CAN:

Y	BEGIN TO DROOL *(EXCESS SALIVATION AIDS SWALLOWING)*
S	BEGIN TO SWALLOW SOLIDS
S	TURN FROM BACK TO SIDE
Y	FOLLOW MOVING OBJECTS WITH EYES
Y	HOLD HEAD ERECT
Y	GURGLE, COO, LAUGH, CRY, & BABBLE
N	SIT WITH SUPPORT FOR UP TO 30 MINUTES
N	ROLL FROM BACK TO STOMACH
Y	USE HANDS TO PUT FOOD INTO MOUTH
N	BEGIN SIGNS OF TEETHING, DROOLING, & CHEWING
Y	MAKE SOUNDS SUCH AS: B, M, D, L, AH, EE, & OO
Y	LOVE REFLECTIONS IN MIRROR
Y	BOUNCE WHEN HELD IN STANDING POSITION
N	SIT UNSUPPORTED FOR A SHORT TIME
Y	GRAB & PLAY WITH FEET
S	DRINK FROM A CUP WITH ASSISTANCE
Y	IMITATE SOME SOUNDS YOU MAKE
Y	DROP THINGS ON PURPOSE
Y	ROLL OVER ONTO STOMACH
Y	USE SIMPLE SOUNDS LIKE: BA, MA, DA, PA, GA

> *Important Note: Infants will develop at similar rates but each in a unique pattern. If you find a baby is not exhibiting the majority of characteristics listed, there could be many plausible reasons ranging from premature birth to a more reserved and cautious personality. This list is a broad overview and not inclusive of all developmental milestones baby will experience.*

BABY _Tonya_	CAREGIVER _Mr. Wang_		DATE _2/6/xx_
Y = YES	S = SOMETIMES	N = NOT YET	

FIGURE 7-4 4-6 Months Developmental Milestones

7–9 Months

DEVELOPMENTAL MILESTONES

BABY CAN:

Y	USE FINGERS TO PICK UP OBJECTS
Y	ROCK WHEN ON HANDS AND KNEES
Y	ADOPT ATTACHMENT TO SPECIAL ITEM
Y	ASSUME A SITTING POSITION
Y	PULL UP TO A STANDING POSITION
Y	HOLD TWO SMALL THINGS, ONE IN EACH HAND
Y	EXPERIENCE STRANGER ANXIETY
Y	PICK UP ITEMS AND PUT IN MOUTH
S	RESPOND TO NAME OR GREETING
Y	BABBLE AS IF SPEAKING A SENTENCE
Y	HOLD A BOTTLE TO DRINK
Y	SCOOT OR CREEP ALONG FLOOR
N	HAVE GREAT PLEASURE EXPLORING OWN BODY
Y	LOVE TO MAKE NOISE WITH OBJECTS
Y	PICK UP SMALL THINGS W/ THUMB & INDEX FINGER
Y	OFTEN START TO CRAWL
S	RESPOND TO A FEW SIMPLE DIRECTIONS/REQUESTS
S	STAND WHEN HAND IS HELD
Y	DRINK FROM A CUP
Y	SHRIEK TO GET ATTENTION
Y	BABBLE, TALK, IMITATE SPEECH SOUNDS
	SIT WITHOUT SUPPORT

> *Important Note: Infants will develop at similar rates but each in a unique pattern. If you find a baby is not exhibiting the majority of characteristics listed, there could be many plausible reasons ranging from premature birth to a more reserved and cautious personality. This list is a broad overview and not inclusive of all developmental milestones baby will experience.*

BABY _Frankie_	CAREGIVER _Ms. Kenmore_	DATE _6/12/xx_

Y = YES	S = SOMETIMES	N = NOT YET

FIGURE 7–5 7–9 Months Developmental Milestones

10–12 Months

DEVELOPMENTAL MILESTONES

BABY CAN:

Y	CRUISE AROUND FURNITURE IN STANDING POSITION
Y	BEGIN TO UNDERSTAND SIMPLE WORDS, DIRECTIVES
Y	BE AFRAID OF LOUD NOISES (*E.G. VACUUM CLEANER*)
Y	START TO MAKE GESTURES (*E.G. BYE-BYE WAVE*)
Y	USE *DA-DA* AND *MA-MA* APPROPRIATELY
N	CLIMB ON CHAIRS
Y	LOOK AT PICTURES IN A BOOK
Y	PLACE OBJECTS IN A CONTAINER & DUMP OUT
S	LIFT LIDS OFF OF CONTAINER TO EXPLORE
Y	DROP AND PICK UP OBJECTS
Y	STAND WITHOUT HELP
Y	BABBLE LONG SOUNDS THAT MAY CONTAIN WORDS
S	ATTEMPT TO ROLL/THROW A BALL BACK TO SOMEONE
Y	USE SIMPLE WORDS: *BALL, DOGGIE, MAMA*
N	WALK WITH LEGS WIDE APART
Y	PREFER TO CRAWL
Y	STAND UP FROM A SQUATTING POSITION
Y	USE A SPOON BUT *NOT CONSISTENTLY*
Y	COOPERATE WITH GETTING DRESSED
Y	PREFER TO FEED SELF
Y	BEGIN TO SCRIBBLE
Y	FIT ONE THING INTO ANOTHER

Important Note: Infants will develop at similar rates but each in a unique pattern. If you find a baby is not exhibiting the majority of characteristics listed, there could be many plausible reasons ranging from premature birth to a more reserved and cautious personality. This list is a broad overview and not inclusive of all developmental milestones baby will experience.

BABY _____Lori_____ CAREGIVER _____Miss Lin_____ DATE _____4/6/xx_____

Y = YES   S = SOMETIMES   N = NOT YET

FIGURE 7–6 10–12 Months Developmental Milestones

4. Place the current age range on an individual clipboard for each infant with the Activities and Play Opportunities, Baby's Monthly Fact Sheet, and Infant Daily Observation Sheet for handy reference when time permits (see Figure 7–7).

The checklist provided is a broad list suggesting approximate developmental milestones that can be expected as outlined for each few months. If you find a baby is not exhibiting the majority of characteristics listed, there could be many reasons. For instance, if the baby was born prematurely then he or she would not be expected to follow the average suggested milestones and might lag a few weeks behind. A baby who is reserved might avoid certain activities but not necessarily to his or her detriment. If you find a baby consistently does not exhibit signs of achieving the majority of the outlined milestones, with a lag of five to seven weeks, then perhaps more exploration is in order; share your concerns with your infant supervisor or nurse consultant for consideration.

Review the developmental milestones when a baby reaches the beginning of the age range. Complete the checklist at the end of the age range. Completing it at the end of the age range provides the baby time to achieve mastery of each skill outlined.

PLANNING ACTIVITIES AND PLAY OPPORTUNITIES

Babies are hard workers. They learn many new skills each month. In order to achieve mastery of each skill, they must be provided with various play opportunities for practice. Since each baby develops at his or her own pace, familiarize yourself with activities that are appropriate for each month of development. Providing a variety of activities will assist a baby to build large and small muscle control, language skills, sensory responses, mental cognition, and social growth. The activities and play opportunities in Figures 7–8 – 7–11 (see pages 79–82) provide a variety of experiences in four areas. Choose activities from all four categories. Circle the corresponding letter next to an activity once the activity is complete. Suggested play opportunities in *The Music of Sound* include exploring sound, music, reading, pictures, and singing to help babies build and master language skills. Exploring and discovering activities listed in *My World* and *Life Is Interesting* provide sensory, and cognitive stimulation. *My Body Is Wonderful* promotes exercise and provides opportunities to use large and small muscles (see Figures 7–8, 7–9, 7–10, and 7–11).

Of course, every day in the infant room is different. Some days a baby will not be in the mood for new activities. A sensitive teacher is careful to avoid overstimulation or sensory overload, especially with the younger infants. When the baby suddenly becomes uninterested, this is a good indication that quiet time is warranted. By gradually introducing new activities, you will continue to create a stimulating environment that is sure to please baby and you!

PRACTICING LANGUAGE SKILLS WITH READING AND SINGING

Children learn language by listening to the sounds around them. Even though infants are unable to talk, they learn by listening to the cooing and talking of their caregivers (Marhoefer & Vadnais 1988). Infants are naturally most tuned into the sound frequency of the human voice. They need to hear talking and the use of descriptive language around them. Scientific research supports the idea that reading, speaking, and singing to babies is crucial to brain development.

Visual stimulation, too, is especially important during the first three to four months, when babies are forming their "sight wiring." Reading to children for as little as 15–20 minutes per day from an early age contributes to a myriad of positive brain developments.

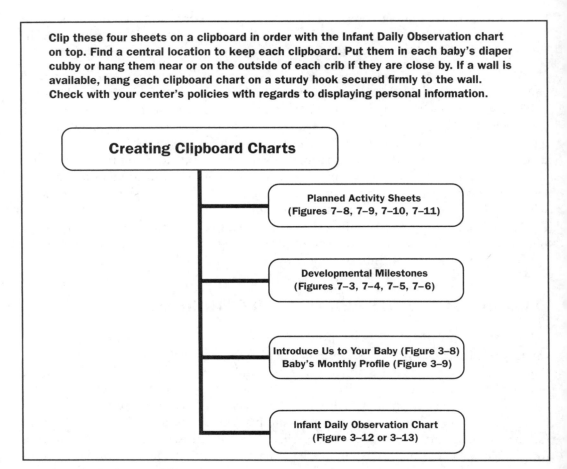

Clip these four sheets on a clipboard in order with the Infant Daily Observation chart on top. Find a central location to keep each clipboard. Put them in each baby's diaper cubby or hang them near or on the outside of each crib if they are close by. If a wall is available, hang each clipboard chart on a sturdy hook secured firmly to the wall. Check with your center's policies with regards to displaying personal information.

Creating Clipboard Charts

Planned Activity Sheets
(Figures 7–8, 7–9, 7–10, 7–11)

Developmental Milestones
(Figures 7–3, 7–4, 7–5, 7–6)

Introduce Us to Your Baby (Figure 3–8)
Baby's Monthly Profile (Figure 3–9)

Infant Daily Observation Chart
(Figure 3–12 or 3–13)

FIGURE 7–7 Clipboard Chart

Snuggle them on your lap and let them point out pictures as you tell the story. Read to them if they are engaged in other floor activities. If the story is too complicated, simplify it and tell the story in your own words. It will be some time before they insist on a story being told verbatim every time it is read!

Use a variety of means to expose babies to language. Short stories are found in books such as *5-Minute Fairy Tales* (1999), written by Publications International. Picture books and vocabulary cards can be found in most education and toy stores such as United Art and Education, 800-322-3247 or http://www.UnitedNow.com. Cut pictures from magazines and place them in a Plexiglas display board, found in school supply catalogs, that attaches to the wall. Change the picture selections on a regular basis. Hang picture mobiles above the diaper changing station (out of baby's reach).

Make a habit of describing your actions to babies. Describe emotions and feelings the babies exhibit. For instance, a baby might cry because he or she is hungry. Respond with, "Yes, you are crying because your stomach is empty and you are hungry. I am warming your bottle now. Let's rock in the chair while we wait." Although babies might not understand immediately, they will eventually make the connection after repeated descriptions. Teaching simple sign language to babies and toddlers is a relatively new trend. It seems very young children are able to understand sign language as a form of communication, and using it lowers frustration for them until they have developed their speech abilities. Several books, videos, and Web sites on the subject are listed under Recommended Resources at the end of the chapter.

1–3 MONTHS

ALL ACTIVITIES 2–10 MINUTES

Activities to assist baby to build:

Large muscle control • Small muscle control • Language skills

Sensory responses • Mental, cognitive, social growth

THE MUSIC OF SOUND

A SHAKE RATTLE
B PLAY MUSIC OR SING JACK & JILL
C HOLD PUPPET & TALK ABOUT NEW FRIENDS
D SHOW & READ SIMPLE PICTURE BOOK
E WIND UP MUSIC BOX & PLACE NEAR BABY
F TALK TO BABY ABOUT THE SEASON OR WEATHER
G PLACE TOYS NEARBY THAT MAKE SOUNDS BY TOUCH
H PLAY A VARIETY OF MUSIC, MUSIC BOXES, OR MUSICAL TOYS
I SING TWINKLE TWINKLE LITTLE STAR
J SHOW PICTURES OF ANIMALS & TALK ABOUT THEM
K CHOOSE BOOKS REFLECTING BABY'S CULTURAL COMMUNITY

MY BODY IS WONDERFUL

A GENTLY MASSAGE LEGS, ARMS, & BACK
B PLACE ON TUMMY, HOLD TOY A FEW INCHES IN FRONT
C AFTER BABY WRAPS FINGERS AROUND YOUR THUMB, MOVE YOUR HAND FROM SIDE TO SIDE
D GENTLY EXPLORE FACE AND EXTREMITIES WITH COTTON BALL
E ROLL BABY GENTLY ONTO SIDE
F GIVE LARGE TOYS TO BE MOUTHED NOT SWALLOWED
G LAY ON TUMMY & PLACE TOYS WITHIN REACH
H LAY ON BACK & ALLOW BABY TO EXPLORE BODY
I HOLD TOY FOR BABY TO REACH & GRASP
J GENTLY MASSAGE BABY'S FEET AND TOES

MY WORLD

A FEELING YOUR BREATH, BLOW THROUGH A STRAW
B PLACE BABY OVER YOUR SHOULDER, SHOW THE SIGHTS
C PLACE BABY IN FRONT OF MIRROR IN PUMPKIN SEAT
D ROCK BABY IN RHYTHM IN ROCKING CHAIR
E SHINE FLASHLIGHT CIRCLES ABOVE BABY'S HEAD
F ALLOW BABY TO WATCH SELF IN MIRROR
G HOLD BABY UP TO WINDOW, TALK ABOUT WHAT YOU SEE
H USE PUPPET/STUFFED ANIMAL, TALK ABOUT SUN/MOON
I TICKLE BABY'S FACE & HANDS WITH SOFT FABRICS
J SIT BABY SUPPORTED, PLAY W/ BRIGHT COLOR BLOCKS

LIFE IS INTERESTING

A HANG, DISCUSS, PICTURES NEAR DIAPER TABLE, CHANGE OFTEN
B PLACE BABY ON BACK & DANGLE TOY IN FRONT
C PROVIDE A MOBILE OR COLORFUL THINGS TO LOOK AT
D SHOW CARDS OF DIFFERENT COLORS
E GENTLY TOUCH SKIN WITH DIFFERENT SOFT FABRICS
F PLAY PEEKABOO, USE BLANKET, SMILE
G LAY BABY ON BACK, GIVE A TRANSPARENT RATTLE
H GIVE BABY A SOFT RUBBER TOY TO SQUEEZE
I STRING BELLS OVER BABY
J GIVE BABY TOY THAT REFLECTS LIGHT/HAS MIRROR

BABY ___Lisa___ CAREGIVER ___Miss Quinn___ DATE ___8/16/xx___

FIGURE 7–8 1–3 Months Activities

4–6 MONTHS

ALL ACTIVITIES 5–10 MINUTES

Activities to assist baby to build:

Large muscle control • Small muscle control • Language skills

Sensory responses • Mental, cognitive, social growth

THE MUSIC OF SOUND

A — MATCH NATURE SOUNDS WITH REAL PICTURES
B — GIVE BABY A TOY THAT SQUEAKS FOR TEETHING
C — PICK A SIMPLE PICTURE BOOK & READ TO BABY
D — SHOW & TALK ABOUT PICTURES OF HOUSEHOLD ITEMS
E — PLAY MUSIC & SING NURSERY RHYMES
F — LISTEN TO RECORDINGS OF BIRD SOUNDS
G — HOLD & SING POP GOES THE WEASEL, LIFT UP ON POP
H — HOLD ON LAP & PLAY PAT-A-CAKE
I — PLAY RECORDED MUSIC FROM MANY CULTURES
J — READ SIMPLE BOOK TO BABY
K — RECITE NURSERY RHYMES OR SIMPLE POETRY
L — READ SIMPLE STORIES USING POP-UP BOOKS
M — PLAY MUSIC WITH STRONG BEAT (E.G. PARADE MUSIC)
N — PLAY PEEKABOO W/SOFT CLOTH, LET BABY PULL OFF
O — SING SONGS, (E.G. HERE WE GO ROUND MULBERRY BUSH)

MY BODY IS WONDERFUL

A — LAY BABY ON BACK, GRASP HANDS & SLOWLY PULL TO SITTING
B — SIT BABY, GENTLY LOWER, REPEAT 6–8 TIMES
C — SIT BABY SUPPORTED, HAND OBJECTS FOR REACHING
D — SIT BABY SUPPORTED, BLOW BUBBLES AROUND BABY
E — HOLD WAIST SECURE, ROLL BACK/FORTH ON BIG BALL
F — SIT ON FLOOR, BABY ON YOUR LEGS TO REACH FOR TOY
G — PUT BABY IN JUMPER SEAT OR BABY BOUNCER
H — PULL BABY BY WAIST TO STAND ON YOUR LAP 3 OR 4 TIMES
I — SIT BABY SUPPORTED, ROLL DIFFERENT BALLS TO BABY
J — LAY ON BACK, GRASP HANDS, SLOW PULL TO SIT & STAND
K — LET BABY GRASP BEADS WHEN CHANGING DIAPER
L — PRACTICE DRINKING SMALL AMOUNTS FROM CUP
M — HAND TOYS BACK & FORTH
N — ALLOW BABY TO PLAY DROP-THE-TOY
O — GIVE 2 OR 3 CUPS THAT FIT INSIDE EACH OTHER

MY WORLD

A — SHOW SEVERAL PICTURES OF HAPPY PEOPLE FACES
B — WALK BABY AROUND ROOM, TALK OF WHAT YOU SEE
C — WALK BABY AROUND ROOM TO TOUCH DIFF. TEXTURES
D — SIT BABY SUPPORTED, GIVE SOFT TOY/ANIMAL TO HUG
E — SHOW FARM ANIMALS & SOUNDS THEY MAKE
F — PUT BABY BY MIRROR TO OBSERVE SELF
G — GIVE A SMALL DAMP WASHCLOTH TO ENJOY
H — SHOW SEVERAL TYPES OF DOG PICTURES
I — GIVE TOYS THAT CREATE NOISES
J — GIVE WASHABLE BRIGHT COLOR PICTURES
K — GIVE SEVERAL TRANSPARENT TOYS TO SEE & DROP
L — GIVE A DISHPAN OF PICTURES
M — GIVE METAL SPOONS IN PAN TO REACH & BANG
N — SIT BABY IN FRONT OF MOUNTED BUSY BOX
O — GIVE STRING OF BIG PLASTIC POP BEADS TO PULL PULL APART

LIFE IS INTERESTING

A — SIT BABY SUPPORTED, ROLL BRIGHT COLORED BALL
B — PLACE BABY ON BACK TO PLAY WITH FLOOR GYM
C — SHOW SEVERAL PICTURES OF DIFFERENT KITTENS
D — TUMMY DOWN, ON BRIGHT COLOR/PATTERN CLOTH/MAT
E — GIVE SEVERAL SIZE RINGS TO HOLD, JIGGLE, CHOMP ON
F — GIVE A VARIETY OF TOYS TO CHEW ON
G — SHOW REAL FLOWERS OR PICTURES
H — BLOW BUBBLES
I — GIVE PAN OF WASHABLE COLOR BLOCKS
J — GIVE SEVERAL RATTLES TO REACH/GRASP
K — PUT DROPS OF WATER IN BABY'S HAND
L — TALK ABOUT PICTURES OF FOOD
M — TALK ABOUT & TOUCH HARD OBJECTS
N — TALK ABOUT & TOUCH SOFT OBJECTS
O — GIVE SMALL WASHABLE BOOKS TO LOOK/CHEW

BABY ___Katrine___ CAREGIVER ___Mr. Santino___ DATE ___12/04/xx___.

FIGURE 7–9 4–6 Months Activities

7–9 MONTHS

ALL ACTIVITIES 5–10 MINUTES

Activities to assist baby to build:

Large muscle control • Small muscle control • Language skills

Sensory responses • Mental, cognitive, social growth

THE MUSIC OF SOUND

A READ & SING NURSERY RHYMES
B PLAY A VARIETY OF MUSIC
C READ TO BABY FROM BOOK ABOUT BABIES
D READ ANIMAL BOOKS & IMITATE SOUNDS
E SING THIS LITTLE PIGGY, USE BABY'S TOES
F HOW MANY EYES, NOSES, MOUTHS, LEGS, FINGERS
G SING JACK & JILL
H PLAY PRE-RECORDED FAMILIAR SOUNDS
I SING EENSY WEENSY SPIDER
J SING OLD MCDONALD
K TALK ABOUT BABY'S TOYS & TEACH THEIR NAMES
L PUT ITEMS IN PAN, ASK BABY TO CHOOSE EACH ITEM
M READ VARIETY OF SIMPLE BOOKS WITH REAL PEOPLE FACES
N HAVE PUPPET TELL BABY ABOUT PUPPET
O PLAY VARIETY OF MUSIC FROM MANY CULTURES

MY BODY IS WONDERFUL

A BOUNCE IN BABY BOUNCER
B HOLD & BOUNCE BABY IN YOUR LAP
C GIVE COLD TEETHING RINGS TO CHEW ON
D HOLD BABY'S OUTSTRETCHED ARMS & WALK
E PLAY PAT-A-CAKE
F BOUNCE BABY IN LAP TO 1 LITTLE, 2 LITTLE, 3 L... BABIES
G ROLL DIFFERENT SIZE BALLS TO BABY
H GENTLY PULL BABY FROM SITTING TO STANDING
I PUT TOY IN POT WITH LID
J HELP BABY TO STAND UP TO/DOWN FROM FURNITURE
K SHOW BABY HOW TO WAVE BYE-BYE
L SHOW BODY PARTS ON DOLL, THEN ON YOUR BODY
M SIT ON FLOOR, TOSS TOY, HAVE BABY CRAWL TO GET IT
N CRAWL WITH BABY, LET BABY PLAY CHASE
O GIVE ITEMS THAT NEST INSIDE EACH OTHER FOR PLAY

MY WORLD

A BOUNCE OR ROCK BABY TO UPBEAT MUSIC
B PLAY PEEKABOO (STILL A FAVORITE)
C FEED BABY WITH A FUZZY SOCK ON BOTTLE
D PLAY WITH SCENTED BOTTLES (SEE EQUIP. LIST)
E PLAY WITH SOAP BUBBLES
F SHOW DESIGN CARDS, LET BABY EXAMINE CARDS
G SIT, CRUMBLE PAPER INTO A BALL, LET BABY CRAWL TO IT
H EXPLORE TEXTURED BOARD BOOKS
I FILL PAN W/ 2" CUBES FOR BABY TO PLAY WITH
J GIVE BABY SOFT DOLLS TO PLAY WITH
K PLAY COPYCAT, BANG SPOON, PAT/TIP HEAD SIDE TO SIDE
L COLOR W/ 1 FAT CRAYON, TAPE PAPER TO HIGHCHAIR TRAY
M SIT & SHOW BABY HOW TO STACK LARGE BLOCKS
N SIT BABY BY MIRROR & TRY ON DIFFERENT HATS
O GIVE PURSE WITH FUN OBJECTS TO EXPLORE

LIFE IS INTERESTING

A DANCE WITH BABY
B LISTEN TO TICK TOCK ON WOUND-UP CLOCK
C LISTEN TO SOUNDS ON BIG BLANKET OUTSIDE
D LAY BABY ON DIFFERENT TEXTURE RUGS TO CRAWL
E TICKLE BABY WITH A FEATHER
F EXPLORE CONTRASTS PROVIDE WARM & COOL WASHCLOTHS
G PUT CLEAN SAFE SIZE ROCKS IN PAN TO EMPTY/FILL
H PLAY WITH TOY TELEPHONE
I PLAY HIDE & SEEK UNDER BLANKET W/ FAMILIAR TOY
J LOOK AT PICTURES OF NATURE
K SWING IN OUTDOOR BABY SWING
L GIVE BABY PANS, LIDS, LARGE PLASTIC SPOONS
M SHOW HOW TO ROCK, PAT, & HUG DOLL
N SHOW PICTURES OF PEOPLE BUSY AT WORK/PLAY
O SHOW HOW TO FEED A DOLL

BABY __Sherry__ CAREGIVER __Miss Verosro__ DATE __2/1/xx__

FIGURE 7–10 7–9 Months Activities

10–12 MONTHS

ALL ACTIVITIES 5–20 MINUTES

Activities to assist baby to build:

Large muscle control • Small muscle control • Language skills
Sensory responses • Mental, cognitive, social growth

THE MUSIC OF SOUND

A ECHO BABY'S SOUNDS & BABBLE BACK TO BABY
B TIE CANNING JAR LIDS TOGETHER FOR BABY TO SHAKE
C READ & LET BABY TURN PAGES OF BOOK
D LET BABY WATCH, LISTEN, TAKE PART IN PUPPET PLAY
E PLAY PARADE, GIVE BABY SPOON & PAN TO BEAT
F CLAP HANDS TO THE MUSIC BEAT
G LOOK AT PICTURE BOOKS WITH EVERYDAY ITEMS
H REPEAT BABY'S WORDS
I GIVE A VARIETY OF BELLS TO RING
J PLAY MUSIC FROM DIFFERENT CULTURES
K GIVE EASY-TO-PLAY MUSIC TOY
L READ BOOKS THAT TELL SIMPLE STORIES
M PLAY MUSICAL INSTRUMENTS
N LOOK AT WORD BOOK WITH MATCHING PICTURES
O SING THE WHEELS ON THE BUS

MY BODY IS WONDERFUL

A GENTLY MASSAGE BABY'S FEET & LEGS
B GENTLY ROLL BABY OVER LARGE BEACH BALL
C PLAY PAT-A-CAKE, HAVE BABY PLAY BACK/CLAP
D HAND UP TO 3 SMALL TOYS TO BABY TO GRASP
E ACT OUT POP GOES THE WEASEL
F CRAWL BEHIND BABY, PLAY CATCH ME
G SHOW HOW TO CRAWL & PUSH A TOY CAR
H PUSH OR RIDE ON PLAY CAR
I SHOW HOW TO REMOVE RINGS FROM STACKING TOY
J GIVE PAN OF COASTERS OR CANNING RINGS
K GIVE LARGE DUPLO BLOCKS TO PUT TOGETHER
L SHOW HOW TO USE SIMPLE SORTER
M SHOW HOW TO PUSH LAWN MOWER/CORN POPPER
N GIVE PULL TOY
O GIVE PUSH CART FULL OF DISHES

MY WORLD

A HAVE BABY DUMP BLOCKS, REMOVE ONE AT A TIME
B PRACTICE STACKING ITEMS
C GIVE BABY A CLEAN WHISK BROOM TO EXPLORE
D SHOW BABY HOW TO PLAY TOY PIANO/XYLOPHONE
E GIVE BABY MILK JUG TO RATTLE & SHAKE
F PLAY PEEKABOO, BABY COVERS OWN EYES
G GIVE LARGE NESTING CUPS FOR PLAY
H GIVE PLASTIC BABY KEYS
I GIVE A PAN W/ LID FULL OF FUN ITEMS
J GIVE A CAN OF TENNIS BALLS
K MAKE STICKY BALLS OF WADDED TAPE TO EXPLORE
L PLAY TEDDY BEAR, TEDDY BEAR
M LIE ON FLOOR, LET BABY CLIMB ON YOU
N BOUNCE BABY ON LAP, SING SONGS
O PLAY WITH BALLS

LIFE IS INTERESTING

A HIDE A TOY UNDER BLANKET FOR BABY TO FIND
B HOLD BABY, PLAY RING-AROUND-THE-ROSY
C SHOW PICTURES OF ANIMALS & PRACTICE SOUNDS
D SHOW HOW TO COVER & ROCK DOLL TO SLEEP
E SIT BY MIRROR, SING ABOUT NOSE, EYES, EARS, MOUTH, HAIR. USE THE TUNE HERE WE GO 'ROUND THE MULBERRY BUSH
F SHOW PICTURES OF FOOD
G SHOW PICTURES OF CLOTHES
H SHOW HOW ITEMS MATCH IN COLOR, SIZE, SHAPE, ETC.
I DROP CLOTHESPINS WITHOUT SPRINGS IN MILK JUG.
J BLOW SOAP BUBBLES FOR BABY
K PLAY DRESS UP
L PLAY ON SIMPLE SLIDE
M STACK FIRM PILLOWS TO CLIMB ON
N SHOW PICTURES OF MODES OF TRANSPORTATION
O PLAY WITH MATCHING PLASTIC, COLORED, BOWLING PINS.

BABY _____*Chris*_____ CAREGIVER _____*Miss Labine*_____ DATE ___*3/7/xx*___ .

FIGURE 7–11 10–12 Months Activities

Singing and playing songs to babies are yet another excellent opportunity for practicing language development. Post the words to songs in your infant room for quick reference (see Figure 7–12). A list such as this is helpful for new teachers and parents who might need a quick refresher. Many resources for infant music are available in catalogs such as:

- *Lullabies* (1966), Compass Productions
- *Sleepy Time Classics for Baby* (2000), Allegro Corporation
- *A Child's Gift of Lullabyes* (1986), by J. A. Brown & D. R. Lehman
  http://www.lullabyes.com

Many infant room rhymes are very old and date as far back as the fourteenth century. Most children love hearing nursery rhymes. Popular nursery rhymes are listed on a Web site called "Lost Lyrics of Old Infant Room Rhymes: 112 Additional Online Infant Room Rhymes, History and their Origins!" http://www.rhymes.org.

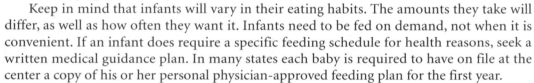

BOTTLE FEEDING AND BURPING PRACTICES

Early feeding experiences can provide a foundation for the development of rich and fulfilling personal relationships. Feeding is an opportunity to provide physical and emotional nourishment. Bottle-feeding is a time to provide each baby with loving acceptance and security. Once you are familiar with each infant's needs and rhythms, you will be able to anticipate their usual feeding time in advance. Follow the procedures outlined in Chapter 5, "Health," to prepare the baby's formula.

Keep in mind that infants will vary in their eating habits. The amounts they take will differ, as well as how often they want it. Infants need to be fed on demand, not when it is convenient. If an infant does require a specific feeding schedule for health reasons, seek a written medical guidance plan. In many states each baby is required to have on file at the center a copy of his or her personal physician-approved feeding plan for the first year.

Always hold babies in an inclined position when feeding them. A bottle-fed baby needs to be held closely and lovingly in the same manner as a breast-fed baby. Smiling, talking, and cuddling are encouraged. Bottle propping is a dangerous practice and deprives a baby of needed physical contact. Every baby has his or her own tempo for eating. Some babies eat rapidly and others eat very slowly. Take care to accommodate each baby's individual eating pattern and allow adequate time to accomplish this task.

Babies are apt to swallow air when they drink so they will need to be bubbled or burped once or twice during a feeding. Place the baby against your chest with his or her head above your shoulder and pat his or her back, gently tapping or rubbing. Another method is to sit the baby upright on your lap with his or her head supported and again pat, or rub his or her back. It is not uncommon for babies to regurgitate a small amount of formula at times. Regurgitation simply means spitting up of small amounts, actually overflowing, perhaps due to an air bubble from rapid nursing or drinking too much milk for the stomach to hold. Vomiting is the expulsion of an appreciable amount of fluid. Although this may also be a result of rapid feeding or inadequate bubbling, it may instead indicate an abnormal condition and requires careful watching.

When the feeding session has ended and the baby is satisfied, provide preventative oral hygiene care. Carefully wipe the baby's teeth and gums with a moistened paper towel to remove any liquid that could contribute to the development of tooth decay. Finally, record the eating session, indicating the time fed and the amount consumed, on the infant's chart.

On a monthly basis update the baby's feeding schedule on the Nutrition Schedule Board covered in Chapter 1 and on the Baby's Monthly Profile covered in Chapter 2. In

SONGS BABIES ENJOY

Hush a Bye Baby (published 1765)

Hush a bye baby, on the tree top,
When the wind blows the cradle will rock;
when the bow breaks, the cradle will fall,
and down will come baby, cradle and all.

Humpty Dumpty (1648)

Humpty Dumpty sat on a wall
Humpty Dumpty had a great fall.
All the King's horses and all the King's men
couldn't put Humpty together again.

Jack & Jill (published 1795)

Jack & Jill went up the hill to fetch a pail of
water. Jack fell down and broke his crown
and Jill came tumbling after.

Hey Diddle Diddle (published 1765)

Hey diddle diddle, the cat and the fiddle,
The cow jumped over the moon. The little
dog laughed to see such a sight and the
dish ran away with the spoon.

Pat-a-Cake (published 1698)

Pat-a-cake, pat-a-cake, baker's man,
Bake me a cake as fast as you can. Pat it,
roll it, and mark it with a B. And put it in the
oven for baby and me.

Jack Be Nimble (published 1798)

Jack be nimble
Jack be quick
Jack jumped over
The candlestick.

Ring Around the Rosy (by Edmund Spenser 1552–1599)

Ring around the rosy, pockets full of posies,
ashes, ashes, we all fall down.

Pop Goes the Weasel (published 1700)

All around the carpenter's bench the monkey
chased the weasel; the monkey stopped to
tie up his shoes, pop goes the weasel.

Hickory, Dickory Dock (published 1744)

Hickory dickory dock
The mouse ran up the clock
The clock struck one
The mouse ran down
Hickory dickory dock

Baa Baa Black Sheep (published 1744)

Baa baa black sheep, have you any wool?
Yes sir, yes, three bags full!
One for the master, one for the dame,
And one for the little boy who lives down the
lane.

This Little Piggy (published 1728)

This little piggy went to the market, this little
piggy stayed home, this little piggy had roast
beef, this little piggy had none, and this little
piggy went wah wah all the way home.

(For additional nursery rhymes online, along
with their history or origin, go to
http://www.rhymes.org.uk)

FIGURE 7-12 Suggested Songs for Babies

your absence a substitute teacher will be able to refer to this current plan at any time for the specific formula, bottle, and nipple type, as well as special feeding arrangements the baby prefers.

PROCURING BABY'S SUPPLIES

Babies require plenty of supplies! If your infant room depends on parents/guardians to provide supplies, use the personal checklist inventory checklist to communicate when supplies need replenishing (see Figure 7–13). Form a habit of reporting the individual inventory once a week. Notify your clients when a baby's supplies are low. Planning ahead will decrease the inconvenience caused by completely depleting needed supplies. Routinely inventory supplies on Thursday or Friday; this allows busy families to shop over the weekend.

BABY'S APPEARANCE AND COMFORT

Keep babies clean and dry at all times. Bibs will help reduce soiling and staining of baby clothing. After a messy lunch, change their clothing. Damp and soiled clothing will encourage rashes to develop in certain areas. Although most infants resist nose wiping, their noses should always remain clean. Help them avoid the discomfort of a nose discharge running down their face and into their mouth. When nose discharges dry and crust around the nostrils, it can cause irritation. Use a disposable, one-use tissue or wipe and then discard it in a plastic-lined, covered, hands-free trash container. To protect yourself, wash your hands after this procedure and often throughout your shift.

BABY'S DEPARTURE

Upon departure there are many details to attend to. Assist the parents/guardians in gathering their baby's belongings, such as soiled clothing, leftover formula, medications, ointments, and blankets, thus promoting a pleasant transition. If time permits, briefly review the daily charting record and add any special observations you might have noted that day. Provide the parents with a copy of this record so they too will have a record of when baby last awoke, ate, and received a diaper change. As you are well aware, babies require a great deal of time and energy. The parents have often spent a long day fulfilling career obligations. Although they are very pleased to see their baby, they often have an accumulation of stress from their day. Your pleasant attitude and helpful manner will allow for a smooth transition from the infant room to home. You have spent a great deal of time caring for their infant. These few extra special moments at the end of a long day will be greatly appreciated and foster feelings necessary to establish trusting relationships.

Early care and learning professionals know that all babies, no matter where they are cared for, deserve the best. In a well-run infant room full of love and joy, the infants develop a strong sense of security and acceptance. You are the primary person who makes that happen. As you bring your day to a close, take a few moments to appreciate yourself for all of the significant efforts and lasting contributions you have made in these little children's lives.

INFANT'S NAME: _____Sydney_____   **DATE:** ____4/09/xx____

SUPPLY	FULL	HALF	NEED MORE
Diapers	✓		
Disposable wipes		✓	
Waterproof paper for diaper barrier (such as wax paper)		✓	
Diaper ointment	✓		
Clothing	✓		
Pacifier/pacifier safety clip	✓		
Bottles		✓	
Nipples			✓
Bottle liners			✓
Jarred food		✓	
Baby cereal	✓		
Other:			

FIGURE 7–13 Personal Supply Inventory Checklist

REFERENCES

Alchin, L. K. Nursery rhymes lyrics and origins. Retrieved October 23, 2004, from http://www.rhymes.org.uk

Clark, A. (2003). *The ABC's of quality child care.* Clifton Park, NY: Thomson Delmar Learning.

Marhoefer, P. E., & Vadnais, L. A. (1988). *Caring for the developing child.* Clifton Park, NY: Thomson Delmar Learning.

RECOMMENDED RESOURCES

Allen, E. K., & Marotz, L. R. *Developmental profiles pre-birth through twelve* (4th ed.) Clifton Park, NY: Thomson Delmar Learning.

Ancona, G., (1989). *Handtalk zoo.* New York: Four Winds Press.

Bourland, B., Cryer, D., & Harms, T. (1987). *Active learning for infants.* Menlo Park, CA: Addison-Wesley Innovative Division.

Collins, S. H. (1994). *An alphabet of animal signs.* Eugene, OR: Garlic Press.

Flodin, M. (1995). *Signing is fun.* New York: Berkley Publishing Group.

Harrington, Co. (1994). ABC Primetime. *From the beginning: Your child's brain.* Los Angeles: American Production.

Joseph, G. (1999). *Sign with your baby: How to communicate with infants before they can speak.* Seattle, WA: Northlight Communications.

Lipson, E. R. (2000). *The New York Times parent's guide to the best books for children.* New York: Three Rivers Press.

McGovern, E. M., & Muller, H. D. (1994). *They're never too young for books.* Buffalo, NY: Prometheus Books.

Rankin, L. (1991). *The handmade alphabet.* New York: Dial Press.

Wheeler, C. (1995). *Simple signs.* New York: Viking.

HELPFUL WEB SITES

Association of American Publishers, Conferences & Publications: Fact Sheet of Importance of Reading to Infants and Young Toddlers. http://www.publishers.org

Bay County Library System. 20 minutes a day. http://www.baycountylibrary.com. Search for 20 minutes a day.

Boston University Erikson Institute. (1998–2001). Brainworks (zero to three). http://zerotothree.org

Brain Development Resources. U.S. Dept. of Education. (2002). *Healthy start grow smart* series. http://www.ed.gov

Brown, A. & Lehman, D. (1986). A Child's Gift of Lullabyes. http://www.lullabyes.com

5-minute Fairy Tales (1999). Lincolnwood, IL: Publications International.

Lullabies (1966). Compass Productions: Arkou Productions.

Reading tips for 20 minutes a day. http://www.aghines.com. Search for reading tips.

Sleepy Time Classics for Baby (2000). Allegro Corporation, http://www.allegro-music.com

WEB SITES FOR SIGN LANGUAGE FOR BABIES

https://www.signingtime.com
https://www.lifeprint.com
https://www.signwithme.com

Educational Articles for Families and Staff

To find your specific State's Licensing, Rules and Regulations go to:

http://nrc.uchsc.edu

This chapter offers a series of educational articles. Post these articles on the current events bulletin board to share information individually, or use them as an educational tool at parent-teacher classes. The articles help staff and parents understand symptoms of common communicable diseases and address topics that are of common concern with children of this age. They are handy to refer to and post, especially when the infant room has experienced an outbreak. An informative approach with the staff and families can significantly reduce cross-infection. The articles include Sudden Infant Death Syndrome, page 89; Colds, page 90; RSV, page 91; Strep Throat, page 92; Ear Infections, page 93; Diarrhea Illness, page 94; Diaper Rash, page 95; Convulsions/Seizures, page 96; and Teething, page 97.

Other books in the KIDEX series contain information on the following:

KIDEX FOR ONES

Impetigo
Pinworms
Ringworm
Provide Toddler Safety
Help Prevent Choking
Is Sharing Possible for Toddlers
Biting Is A Toddler Affair

KIDEX FOR TWOS

Mashed Fingers
Chicken Pox
Scabies
Submersion and Drowing Accidents
Tooth Injuries
Temper Tantrums
Toilet Training
Dental Care for Young Children

KIDEX FOR THREES

Vision Screening
Learning from the Process, Not the Outcome
Conducting a Cooking Class for
    Three-Year-Olds
Whining Is a Form of Communication
Questions About Hearing for Young Children
When Does the Learning Start?
Pink Eye

KIDEX FOR FOURS

Is My Child Ready for Kindergarten?
Healthy "Floor Posture"
Bedwetting
My Child Is Shy
Signs of Child Abuse
Styles of Learning
My Child Stutters!

SUDDEN INFANT DEATH SYNDROME (SIDS)

Sudden Infant Death Syndrome (SIDS) is defined as the unexpected and sudden death of an appaently healthy infant during sleep with no evidence of disease (Rothenberg & Chapman 1994). SIDS is the leading cause of death in babies after the first month of life. The National Back to Sleep Campaign recommends that placing babies on their back can reduce the risk of SIDS (US Dept of Health & Human Services 1997). Although the exact cause is unknown, many risk factors have been linked to an increased incidence of the syndrome.

The Back to Sleep Campaign recommends several measures for reducing the risk of SIDS.

- Back sleeping is the best position.
- Inform and educate all family members and caregivers who care for your baby.
- Use a firm mattress.
- Avoid soft mattresses, sofas, sofa cushions, waterbeds, sheepskins, bean bag chairs, or other soft surfaces.
- Make sure baby's face and head stay uncovered during sleep.
- Don't smoke before or after the birth of baby.
- Avoid second-hand smoke environments.
- Keep your baby warm during sleep but do not overheat. Too many blankets and clothes can overheat your baby.
- Seek consistent health care throughout your pregnancy and follow-up well-baby care for your infant.
- Breast-feed your baby if possible to pass on "natural immunities" that reduce illness during the first year.

Plan "tummy time" when baby is awake and you are able to observe. Regular tummy time during awake periods promotes the development of stronger neck and shoulder muscles. Flat spots (plagiocephaly) often develop from extended periods of back sleeping. It is a temporary condition that disappears when baby begins to sit up.

References

Back to Sleep Campaign / National Institute of Child Health and Human Development. http://www. keepkidshealthy.com/welcome/safety/ back_to_sleep.html

Rothenberg, M., & Chapman, C. (1994). *Dictionary of medical terms* (3rd ed.). New York: Barron's.

US Dept of Health and Human Services. (1997). *Sudden Infant Death Syndrome; Back to Sleep Campaign.* Retrieved December 12, 2004, from http://www.crn.org/sids/sleep.thm

Resources

Sudden Infant Death Syndrome: Sudden Infant Death Syndrome (SIDS) is the diagnosis given for the sudden death of an infant under one year of age that remains unexplained after a complete investigation. Because most cases of SIDS occur when a baby is sleeping in a crib, SIDS is also commonly known as crib death.

Infant Sleep Positioning and SIDS: Tips to reduce the risk of SIDS from the American Academy of Pediatrics

Association of SIDS and Infant Mortality Programs: Infant Sleeping Positioning and SIDS: Counseling Implications and other risk reduction recommendations to prevent SIDS.

SIDS Alliance–Back to Sleep: A national, nonprofit, voluntary health organization dedicated to the support of SIDS families, education, research, and information about the Back to Sleep Campaign to reduce the risk of SIDS.

COLDS

There are more than 200 viruses that cause the common cold (Time-Life 1996, 280). Colds are not caused by sleeping near an open window, having damp feet, or being in the wind without a hat. Viral germs are spread easily in the closed living conditions we often experience in the winter months. Because so many different viruses cause colds, there will probably never be one vaccine to prevent them. Due to their in completely developed immune systems, children are more susceptible to infections.

Symptoms of a cold include

- runny nose
- nasal congestion
- noisy breathing
- redness around the nose, eyes, or throat
- aches and pains
- headaches
- chills
- decreased appetite
- listlessness
- cough
- fever

Most colds can be effectively treated with rest and fluids. Our bodies have the ability to heal themselves. Note that medicines available on the market will only relieve symptoms. They will not cure or shorten a cold's duration. Antibiotics kill only bacteria and have no effect on cold viruses. Sometimes antibiotics are given to prevent a secondary infection by bacteria (Black & Mattassarin-Jacobs 1997). When should a child be treated by medical personnel for a cold?

It is advisable to seek medical advice if

- a fever is over 103°F or 39.4°C
- sore throat or sore glands are present in the neck
- ear pain or ear drainage develops
- a stiff neck or sore back is present
- shortness of breath, wheezing, or trouble breathing occurs
- cold symptoms exceed 7–10 days
- a child is too sick to drink (*Kemper 1996, 100*)
- a persistent cough interferes with rest

References

Editors of Time-Life Books. (1996). *The medical advisor: The complete guide to alternative & conventional treatments.* Alexandria:Time-Life.

Black, J., & Mattassarin-Jacobs, E. (1997). *Medical surgical nursing* (5th ed.). Philadelphia: Saunders.

Kemper, K.J. (1996). *The holistic pediatrician.* New York: HarperPerennial.

RSV (RESPIRATORY SYNCTIAL VIRUS)

RSV is a common virus and the most frequent cause of colds and breathing problems in children under the age of three. It is highly contagious and "virtually all children get RSV disease within the first two years of life." Children under the age of one generally require medical intervention when experiencing RSV. High-risk children who are infected with RSV disease often need to be hospitalized (Protecting Your Child from RSV, Which Babies Are at Risk?) In older children and adults the symptoms may be very mild.

Symptoms of RSV include

- runny nose
- extreme nasal stuffiness and a runny nose that interferes with sleep
- pharyngitis—inflammation or infection of the pharynx, usually producing a sore throat
- persistent coughing and sneezing
- wheezing
- possible ear or eye infection (Time-Life 1996)
- continuous low-grade fever
- difficult or rapid breathing
- poor appetite

If a child is hospitalized with RSV, it is usually for breathing treatments to help open his or her airway and assist with mucus removal. Once a child has experienced RSV, any repeated infections usually are milder than the first time. The highest incidence of RSV generally occurs from late fall to spring. Diligent hand washing, regular toy and equipment sanitation, and fresh air reduce the spread of germs and viruses. Keep your high-risk infant from others experiencing cold symptoms, and avoid exposing him or her to cigarette smoke.

References

Editors of Time-Life Books. (1996). *The medical advisor: The complete guide to alternative & conventional treatments.* Alexandria: Time-Life.

RSVprotection.com. *Protecting your child from RSV, Which babies are at risk?* Retrieved November 20, 2004, from http://www.rsvprotection.com/which.htm

STREP THROAT

Strep throat is caused by group A Streptococcus bacteria. Strep throat is usually spread by an infected person who coughs or sneezes contaminated droplets into the air or from touching contaminated secretions.

Symptoms of strep throat include

- severe sore throat
- fever
- headache
- swollen glands

If not treated, strep infections can lead to scarlet fever (bright red, textured body rash), rheumatic fever (a serious disease that can damage heart valves), pneumonia, and bloodstream and ear infections. Strep infections are treated with antibiotics. A child who has been treated with antibiotic therapy and has had no fever for at least 24 hours can generally return to the child care facility.

Resource

National Institutes of Health. US Department of Health and Human Services. Health Matters. http://www.niad.nih.gov/

EAR INFECTIONS

Ear infections now account for 25 percent of all doctor visits for children under the age of five years old. Actually the infection is in the middle ear and is referred to as otitis media. Bacteria and fluids invade the middle ear. Ear infections almost always hurt (Kemper 1996,180). Pain often increases when the child lies down. Blood flow increases to the head, resulting in more pressure in the ear causing a throbbing sensation. Occasionally a child may show no symptoms at all. Babies often exhibit fussy behavior and touch the affected ear in a "batting motion." Another telltale sign a child exhibits is suddenly awakening from a sound sleep and crying frantically. Fluid builds up in the affected ear, causing pressure and severe pain. Ear infections often require antibiotic therapy to eliminate the bacterial invasion. Complicated ear infections can lead to more serious conditions such as a ruptured ear drum and potential hearing loss. After the bacterial infection is cleared, it is common for fluid to persist for several weeks or months.

PREVENTION MEASURES

During the winter months more infections occur because we are shut indoors and share our space more closely with others. Reducing the potential spread of infection is well worth the effort in a group child care setting. Take the time to prepare for this season by directing your attention to matters aimed for prevention.

To prevent the spread of infection

- Encourage the children to contain their coughs and sneezes with a tissue.

- Promote good hand washing practices among staff and children.

- Do not crowd naptime cots, and place the children's heads opposite each other.

- Make sure the rooms are well ventilated.

- Clean and disinfect all common surfaces and toys daily.

- Reduce eating mucus-producing foods such as dairy.

- When feeding an infant, avoid allowing "milk dribble" to enter the ear. (This can occur toward the end of the feeding if the infant falls asleep.)

- Dress yourself and the children appropriately and take them outdoors several times a day for fresh air and exercise.

It is not necessary to exclude a child with a cold from your program, if he or she can participate comfortably and does not require one-on-one care. Such exclusion is of little benefit since viruses have often been spread prior to the appearance of symptoms. A runny nose that lasts for weeks or months is more likely an allergy than a virus.

Parents can help reduce the occurrence of colds by assuring their children receive adequate rest and eat a well-balanced diet with vegetables and fruit rich in vitamin C. It is especially important to avoid exposing children to second-hand smoke from cigarettes.

Research continues to support the idea that we often overtreat cold symptoms. Avoid the use of over-the-counter cold remedies without medical guidance. It is helpful to remember that treated or not, most colds resolve on their own within seven to 10 days.

Give attention to these suggested prevention methods as part of your ongoing program. By practicing these preventions daily, you will promote a healthy environment for the little ones you care for.

Reference

Kemper, K.J. (1996). *The holistic pediatrician.* New York: HarperPerennial.

DIARRHEA ILLNESS

How Do I Know This Is Diarrhea?

There are two signs that, in general, help you to identify diarrhea.

1. NUMBER OF STOOLS: An increase in the number of bowel movements that the child usually has in a day or in a few hours. (Example: Two loose stools from a child who usually has one formed stool a day.)

2. SHAPE OF STOOLS: The stool changes in "shape" and is not formed or becomes soft or liquid. (Exception: Breast-fed babies have loose stools.)

What Is Considered Abnormal?

Any of the following are abnormal: bloody stool, mucus in stool, watery diarrhea, sudden loss of control, abdominal cramps, loss of appetite, fever, nausea, excessive lethargy or sleepiness, vomiting.

Any of these symptoms may occur in association with diarrhea or before the diarrhea begins. When diarrhea is happening to a child it is called "diarrhea illness" and may spread to others easily.

What Should Be Done When Abnormal Stools Occur?

Notify the parent or guardian, separate the child from the other children to prevent possible spread, and send the child home.

Help Yourself And The Children In Your Care: Call your county health department to report two or more children with a diarrhea illness.

PREVENT THE SPREAD OF DISEASE IN YOUR CHILD CARE FACILITY
IMPORTANT FACTS ABOUT DIARRHEA

Remember, diarrhea is stools that are watery or loose and occur more often than normal for the individual child. One newborn may have 7–10 stools a day, whereas another might have stools only every other day. Both may be normal if that is usual for that baby.

1. The stools are very bad smelling or there is blood or mucus in the stool. (An occasional green stool is not harmful.)

2. The diarrhea is accompanied by a fever.

3. The child seems overly tired or does not act "right." (e.g., too sleepy or too fussy).

4. The child has less urine, seems to have a dry mouth, or does not have tears when crying.

5. There is severe stomach pain.

6. The baby is under a year old.

7. The diarrhea does not get better.

Resources

Center for Disease Control and Prevention (CDC). http://www.cdc.gov
E. Coli 0157 : H7Infection. http://www.in.gov.isdh

DIAPER RASH

Most diaper rashes are due to a combination of heat, moisture, and chemical irritants (feces, urine, detergents, etc.) that become trapped in the diaper area and cause irritation of the skin. Scipien, Barnard, Chard, Howe, Phillips (1975) report that ammonia dermatitts, caused by the breakdown of urea in the urine to ammonia by bacteria in the feces presents a similar clinical picture. The skin appears shiny, red, and excoriated (p. 827–828). Occasionally a fungus or bacteria will take advantage of the irritated skin, and an infection occurs. The best plan is to prevent the rash by keeping the diaper area clean and dry as much of the time as possible. When this fails and a rash is noted, use the following guidelines.

Diaper area with red, irritated skin:

1. Change diapers frequently.
2. Wash the diaper area with a mild soap, rinse well with clear water, and pat the skin dry.
3. Allow the skin to air dry for 10–15 minutes; then, before diapering, apply a thin layer of a protective physician-ordered ointment or cream. Wear latex gloves if skin is cracked and broken open.
4. Do not use cornstarch or powders.
5. If the rash worsens or if it does not improve after four to five days of treatment, seek medical attention.

Diaper area with red or yellow bumps or areas of raw, oozing skin:

These signs could indicate a rash that needs medical treatment.
Recommend that the parents seek medical evaluation.

Reference

Scipien, G. M., Barnard, M. U., Chard, M. A., Howe, J., & Phillips, P. J. (1975). *Comprehensive pediatric nursing.* New York: McGraw-Hill.

CONVULSIONS/SEIZURES

A convulsion or seizure is an involuntary, automatic, not consciously willed movement. It is not uncommon in young children who have a fever. It can also be caused by epilepsy, though this is less common than a fever related seizure. Kemper (1996) reports that sometimes between the ages of three months and five years, about 3 to 5 percent of children have seizures when they have a fever. This is not epilepsy (p. 207). Seizures may be mild or severe. Those related to fever are usually more severe than epileptic seizures.

A convulsive child may thrash about in jerking motions, lose consciousness, drool, urinate, or have a bowel movement. Frequently his or her eyes seem to roll up into the head. A mild seizure may consist of a staring, glassy-eyed, blank, or absent spell.

1. Ease the convulsive child to the floor, if possible. Do not try to restrain him or her.

2. Remove hard or dangerous objects from the immediate area.

3. Turn the child's head to the side to allow the saliva to drain.

4. Allow the child to sleep after a seizure. Give no food or liquids until he or she is fully alert.

5. Do not leave the child alone.

Call the parents immediately so they may contact their physician. Though a convulsion is frightening to onlookers, it is generally not harmful. If breathing should stop (it rarely does), administer rescue breathing and call for emergency assistance. Always call the doctor after a seizure is over. An examination is usually necessary. Call 9-1-1 or the appropriate EMS number if the seizure lasts more than two minutes. If you call 9-1-1 when the seizure begins, you are not overreacting.

Reference

Kemper, K.J. (1996). *The holistic pediatrician.* New York: HarperPerennial.

TEETHING

A baby's first tooth may appear as early as three months or not until after the first birthday. There is a wide variation in the normal eruption cycle (Fisher 1988). Once the process has occurred teeth will erupt periodically until around three years of age. Teething symptoms and discomfort also vary from baby to baby. Many babies exhibit little or no discomfort; others are quite fussy and irritable and drool profusely (Johnson 2004). Babies will probably have an increased desire to chew. Many safe teething rings are on the market, and babies might especially enjoy chewing on rings that are chilled. Avoid the teething rings that have fluid and objects in them. Choose solid rings. It is important to note that there are many misconceptions with regard to teething symptoms. An ongoing debate exists among health professionals that would argue that teething does not cause cold symptoms or diarrhea, nor does "teething raise the temperature above 101°F (38.4°C)" (Jaber, Cohen, & Mor 1992). They feel loose stools are often caused by swallowing excessive saliva. Since diarrhea is caused by bacterial or viral illness, they might argue it is not caused by teething. Yet one pediatrician (Johnson 2004) noted an usual scenario that a parent will bring in an irritable six-month-old who has a low-grade fever (less than 100.5°F) and some mild diarrhea exhibiting signs of drooling and chewing. . . then two or three days later a new tooth appears and the fever and diarrhea disappear.

References

Fisher, J. (1988). *From baby to toddler: Month-by-month resource on your child's first two years of life*, New York: Berkely.

Jaber, L., Cohen, I. J., Mar, A., *Fever associated with teething. Archives of Disease in Childhood:* 233–234 Retrieved February 6, 1992, from http://ncbi.nlm.nih.gov/
entrez/query.fcgi?cmd=Retrieve&db=PubMed&list_uids=1543387&dopt=A

Johnson. (2004). *Baby teeth: Frequently asked questions.* Retrieved October 10, 2004, from
http://www.americanbaby.com/ab/printablestory.jhtml?storyid=
templatedata/ab/story/data/11021.xml&ca

RECOMMENDED ARTICLES AND WEB-SITES FOR PARENT EDUCATION

Birth to Three—A nonprofit organization that provides parenting education and support to families with young children. Offers parenting curriculum for families with chidren from infancy through age three. Includes group leader manual, session modules, booklets, activities, handouts, and graduation certificates: http://www.birthto3.org

Common colds for young children. Excerpt Shelov, S.P., MD, FAAP & Hannemann, R.E., MD, FAAP, Caring for your baby and young child: Birth to age 5 (4th ed.). American Academy of Pediatrics. Retrieved from http://www.aap.org

Separation anxiety. Excerpt from Shelov, S.P., MD, FAAP & Hannemann, R.E., MD, FAAP, *Caring for your baby and young child: Birth to age 5* (4th ed.). American Academy of Pediatrics. Retrieved from http://www.aap.org

Thumb sucking and pacifiers. Excerpt from Shelov, S.P., MD, FAAP & Hannemann, R.E., MD, FAAP, *Caring for your baby and young child: Birth to age 5* (4th ed.). American Academy of Pediatrics. Retrieved from http://www.aap.org

RECOMMENDED RESOURCES

Conner, B. (2000). *Everyday opportunities for extraordinary parenting (Rev.ed.)* Naperville, IL: Sourcebooks.

VanGorp, L. (2001) *1001 Best website for parentings.* Westminister, CA: Teacher Created Materials.

Index

To find your specific
State's Licensing, Rules
and Regulations go to:

http://nrc.uchsc.edu

APPENDIX

Forms and Templates

A

Organized by chapter this appendix contains the following forms and templates for your convenience.

Cleaning Schedule

For the Week of _____

Classroom _____

Daily Cleaning Projects	Mon	Tue	Wed	Thr	Fri	Once A Week Projects	Initial	Date
1. Mop floors						Scrub brush & mop (corners)		
2. Clean all sinks (use cleanser)						Wipe down all bathroom walls		
3. Wipe down walls (around sinks)						Scrub step stools		
4. Clean & disinfect toilets (with brush in & out)						Use toothbrush on fountain (mouth piece)		
5. Clean water fountains/wipe with disinfectant						Clean windows		
6. Clean inside of windows and seals						Wipe off door handles		
7. Clean inside & outside glass on doors						Organize shelves		
8. Clean & disinfect changing table & under the pad						Move furniture and sweep		
9. Run vacuum (carpet & rugs)						Wipe underneath tables & legs		
10. Dispose of trash (replace bag in receptacle)						Wipe chair backs and legs		
11. Wipe outside of all cans & lids with disinfectant						Wipe off cubbies/shelves		
12. Repeat 10 & 11 for diaper pails						**Immediate Project**		
13. Clean & disinfect high chairs/tables/chairs						Any surface area contaminated with body fluids		
14. Clean & disinfect baby beds/cots						such as blood, stool, mucous, vomit or urine		
15. Reduce clutter! (Organize!)						**Carpet Cleaning-Quarterly**		
16. (infant & toddler groups) Wipe/sanitize toys after each individual use								
17. Change crib sheets as directed								
18.								

Lead Teacher: _____   C – Complete   N/A – Not Applicable

Nutrition Schedule Bulletin Board

								Baby's Name
								Breakfast/ Beverage
								Snack/ Beverage
								Lunch/ Beverage
								Snack/ Beverage
								Dinner/ Beverage
								Snacks
								Bottle Type
								Nipple Type
								Pacifier

KIDEX
for
INFANTS

_____

BABY'S NAME

_____

YEAR

KIDEX *for* INFANTS
Class Book

_____
GROUP NAME

INFANT ROOM ENROLLING APPLICATION

Child's Full Name: _____ Nickname: _____

Date of Birth: _____ Sex: _____ Home Phone: _____

Address: _____ City: _____ Zip Code: _____

Legal Guardian: _____

Mother's Name: _____ Home Phone: _____

Address: _____ City: _____ Zip Code: _____

Employer: _____ Work Phone: _____

Address: _____ City: _____ Zip Code: _____

Father's Name: _____ Home Phone: _____

Address: _____ City: _____ Zip Code: _____

Employer: _____ Work Phone: _____

Address: _____ City: _____ Zip Code: _____

IN THE EVENT YOU CANNOT BE REACHED IN AN EMERGENCY, CALL:

Name: _____ Relationship: _____ Phone: _____

Address: _____ City: _____ Zip Code: _____

Name: _____ Relationship: _____ Phone: _____

Address: _____ City: _____ Zip Code: _____

OTHER PEOPLE RESIDING WITH BABY

Name: _____ Relationship: _____ Age: _____

Name: _____ Relationship: _____ Age: _____

Name: _____ Relationship: _____ Age: _____

PEOPLE AUTHORIZED TO REMOVE BABY FROM THE NURSERY

Your baby will not be allowed to go with anyone unless their name appears on this application, or you provide them with an "authorization card," or you make other arrangements with the management. Positive I.D. will be required.

Name: _____ Relationship: _____

Name: _____ Relationship: _____

Name: _____ Relationship: _____

Baby Will Attend: Mon - Tues - Wed - Thur - Fri - Sat - Sun

Baby Will Be: Full Time or Part Time

Time Child Will Be Dropped Off (Normally): _____

Time Child Will Be Picked Up (Normally): _____

MEDICAL INFORMATION/AUTHORIZATION

Physician's Name: _____ Phone: _____

Address: _____ City: _____ Zip Code: _____

Dentist's Name: _____ Phone: _____

Address: _____ City: _____ Zip Code: _____

Allergies: _____

I agree and give consent that, in case of accident, injury, or illness of a serious nature, my child will be given medical attention/emergency care. I understand I will be contacted immediately, or as soon as possible if I am away from the numbers listed on this form.

PERMISSION TO LEAVE PREMISES

I hereby give the nursery _____ permission to take my child on

neighborhood walks using a _____ (state equipment, e.g., a

baby buggy that seats six children & has safety straps). YES _____   (INITIAL)

NO, I do not give permission at this time: _____   (INITIAL)

Parent/Guardian's Signature: _____

Parent/Guardian's Signature: _____

Date: _____

AUTHORIZED
PERSON
CARD

AUTHORIZED
PERSON
CARD

AUTHORIZED
PERSON
CARD

AUTHORIZED
PERSON
CARD

AUTHORIZED
PERSON
CARD

AUTHORIZED
PERSON
CARD

AUTHORIZED
PERSON
CARD

AUTHORIZED
PERSON
CARD

AUTHORIZED
PERSON
CARD

AUTHORIZED
PERSON
CARD

USE HEAVY CARD STOCK (FRONT OF CARD)

Name of Authorized Person

May pick up my child _____

on my behalf.

Parent/Guardian Signature   Date

Name of Authorized Person

May pick up my child _____

on my behalf.

Parent/Guardian Signature   Date

Name of Authorized Person

May pick up my child _____

on my behalf.

Parent/Guardian Signature   Date

Name of Authorized Person

May pick up my child _____

on my behalf.

Parent/Guardian Signature   Date

Name of Authorized Person

May pick up my child _____

on my behalf.

Parent/Guardian Signature   Date

Name of Authorized Person

May pick up my child _____

on my behalf.

Parent/Guardian Signature   Date

Name of Authorized Person

May pick up my child _____

on my behalf.

Parent/Guardian Signature   Date

Name of Authorized Person

May pick up my child _____

on my behalf.

Parent/Guardian Signature   Date

Name of Authorized Person

May pick up my child _____

on my behalf.

Parent/Guardian Signature   Date

Name of Authorized Person

May pick up my child _____

on my behalf.

Parent/Guardian Signature   Date

USE HEAVY CARD STOCK (BACK OF CARD)

Introduce Us to Your Baby

Baby's Name:_____ Nickname:_____ Date of Birth:_____

Father's Name:_____ Mother's Name:_____

Siblings' Names & Ages:_____

SLEEPING PATTERNS:

1. How does your baby show you he or she is ready for sleep? _____

2. How do you prepare baby for nap? (rocking, swinging, etc.) _____

Time	Napping Approx. how long?	Time	Indicate Food & Formula

EATING PATTERNS:

1. Name of formula currently using: _____

2. Are you currently breast-feeding? _____

3. What type of bottles and nipples do you use? _____

4. Do you feed your baby water? If so, how often? _____

5. Are there any eating difficulties? _____

6. Has your baby started cereal? If yes, how often and how much? _____

7. Does your baby have any allergies?_____

8. Do you wish for your baby to feed on demand? _____

9. Does your baby take a pacifier? _____ Type: _____

10. How does your baby indicate he or she is hungry? _____

11. Do you have any nutrition concerns we should be aware of? _____

ELIMINATION PATTERNS:

1. How often do you change your baby's diaper at home? _____

2. How frequently does your baby eliminate B.M. stools? _____

3. What is the usual color or consistency of the stool? _____

HEALTH PATTERNS:

1. Does your baby regularly take medications? _____ If yes, please indicate the
   type, amount, and time it is given: _____

2. Are there any health problems or handicaps?_____ If yes, please state specifically:

   _____

ACTIVITY PATTERNS:
At what age did your child begin creeping? _____ crawling? _____ walking?_____

STRESS/COPING PATTERNS:

Describe your baby's teething symptoms: _____

Is there any other information we should know that will help us get acquainted with your baby?

_____

_____

_____

_____

_____

_____

_____

List all names of people authorized to take your baby from the center:_____

_____

Baby will attend: MON TUE WED THUR FRI SAT SUN Start Date: _____

Time baby will normally arrive: _____ depart: _____

Person completing interview: _____

Parent / Guardian Signature: _____

Parent / Guardian Signature: _____

** In order to assure a smooth transition, this completed form must accompany baby when care is initiated.**

BABY'S MONTHLY PROFILE

Month: _____ Caregivers: _____

Baby's name: _____ Birth date: _____ Age: _____

Parents' /Guardians' names: _____

Personality Traits: shy/reserved   outgoing/curious   sensitive/frightens easily
(Circle all that apply)   very verbal   active   restless
                       cuddly   demonstrative   stranger anxiety
                       cautious

Parent's Concerns/Instructions: _____

Health Concerns: _____

Daily Medications: yes _____   no _____ (see med sheet for details)

Allergies: _____

Ointment Used: _____

Special Nap Instructions: _____

Usual Nap times   _____to _____   _____to _____

Pacifier Type: _____   Bottle/Nipple Type: _____

Formula Name: _____   Amount: _____

Baby's Eating Schedule:

Breakfast	Snack/Beverage	Lunch	Snack/Beverage	Dinner	Snack/Beverage
_____	_____	_____	_____	_____	_____
_____	_____	_____	_____	_____	_____

Days Attending: Mon   Tue   Wed Thur Fri   Sat   Sun

Approx. Arrival: _____   Approx. Departure: _____

Those authorized to pick up: _____
_____

Warning: If name is not listed, consult with office and obtain permission to release child. If you are not familiar with this person, always request I.D.

Daily Infant Schedule

Early Morning	
Mid Morning	
Late Morning	
Mid Day	
Early Afternoon	
Mid Afternoon	
Late Afternoon	
Early Evening	

Infant Daily Observation Checklist

Infant's name: _____ Date: _____

Arrival: _____ Departure: _____

	Time	Ate Partial	Ate Complete	Oz Juice	Oz Water	Oz Breast Milk	Oz Formula	Cereal	Fruits	Meat/ Protein	Vegetable	Crackers/ Bread
Breakfast												
Snack												
Lunch												
Snack												
Dinner												
Snack												

Nap Times: _____ _____ _____ _____

Diaper Changes				
Time	**Wet**	**BM**	**Dry**	**Initials**

	Medications*	Treatments*
Time		
Time		
Time		

*See Daily Medication Sheet for Details

Moods / Activity Level:
Circle all that apply
Busy • Curious • Adventurous
Cheerful • Quiet • Content • Cuddly
Drowsy • Bubbly • Verbal/Babbling
Periods of Fussiness • Grumpy

Comments: _____
_____
_____
_____
_____

Primary Caregiver: _____ Shift Time: _____

Caregiver: _____ Shift Time: _____

INFANT DAILY OBSERVATION SHEET

Arrival Time:		WET-BM		2:30		WET-BM
6:30				3:30		
7:30				4:30		
8:30				5:30		
9:30				6:00		
10:30				Comments:		
11:30						
12:30						
1:30				Departure Time:		

Baby's Name _____

Date _____ M T W TH F S S

Primary Caregiver _____

INFANT DAILY OBSERVATION SHEET

Arrival Time:		WET-BM		2:30		WET-BM
6:30				3:30		
7:30				4:30		
8:30				5:30		
9:30				6:00		
10:30				Comments:		
11:30						
12:30						
1:30				Departure Time:		

Baby's Name _____

Date _____ M T W TH F S S

Primary Caregiver _____

Diaper Changing Procedures for Disposable Diapers

Supplies: Disposable nonabsorbent gloves, nonabsorbent paper liner disposable wipes removed from container, child's personally labeled ointments (under medical direction) diapers, cotton balls, plastic bags, tissues, physician-prescribed lotions, lidded hands-free plastic-lined trash container, soap, disinfectant, and paper towels.

Use a nonabsorbent changing surface. Avoid dangerous falls: keep a hand on baby at all times and never leave alone. In emergency, put child on floor or take with you.

	Steps for Changing Disposable Diapers				
1	Wash hands with soap and water.	2	Gather supplies.	3	Put on disposable waterproof gloves (if used).
4	Cover diapering surface with nonabsorbent paper liner.	5	Place baby on prepared diapering area (minimize contact: hold baby away from your body if extremely wet or soiled).	6	Put soiled clothes in a plastic bag.
7	Unfasten diaper. Leave soiled diaper under the child.	8	Gently wash baby's bottom. Remove stool and urine from front to back, and use a fresh wipe each time. Dispose directly in designated receptacle.	9	Fold soiled diaper inward and place in designated receptacle followed by the disposable gloves (if used).
10	Use disposable wipe to clean surface of caregiver's hands and another to clean the child's.	11	Check for spills on paper. If present, fold over so fresh part is under buttocks.	12	Place clean diaper under baby.
13	Using a cotton ball or tissue, apply skin ointment to clean, dry area if indicated/ordered.	14	Fasten diaper and dress with fresh clothing.	15	Wash baby's hands with soap and water between 60°F and 120°F for 15–20 sec. and dry. Turn faucet off with a paper towel, then place baby in a safe location.
16	Clean and disinfect diapering area, leaving bleach solution in contact at least 2 minutes. Allow table to air dry, or wipe it after 2 minutes.	17	Wash your hands with soap and water for at least 15–20 seconds. Turn off faucet with paper towel.	18	Chart diaper change and any observations.

Adapted from: Standard 3.014 Diaper changing procedure. Caring for our children, National health and safety performance standards (2nd ed.) Used with permission, American Academy of Pediatrics. Permission to photocopy is granted by Thomson Delmar Learning.

Diaper Changing Procedures for Cloth Diapers

Supplies: Disposable nonabsorbent gloves, non absorbent paper liner, disposable wipes removed from container, child's personally labeled ointments (under medical direction), diapers, cotton balls, plastic bags, tissues, physician-prescribed lotions, lidded hands-free plastic-lined trash container, soap, disinfectant, and paper towels.

Soiled Diapers: *Contain in a labeled and washable plastic-lined receptacle that is tightly lidded and hands-free only. Don't require separate bags. However, any soiled diapers sent home are to be secured in a plastic bag, separately bagged from soiled clothing. Clean and disinfect receptacle daily and dispose of waste water in toilet or floor drain only.*

Use a nonabsorbent changing surface. Avoid dangerous falls: keep a hand on baby at all times and never leave alone. In emergency, put child on floor or take with you.

Steps for Changing Cloth Diapers								
1	Wash hands with liquid soap and water.	2	Gather supplies.	3	Put on disposable waterproof gloves (if used).			
4	Cover diapering surface with nonabsorbent paper liner.	5	Place baby on prepared diapering area (minimize contact: hold baby away from your body if extremely wet or soiled).	6	Put soiled clothes in a plastic bag.			
7	Unfasten diaper. Leave soiled diaper under the child. Close each safety pin immediately out of child's reach. Never hold pins in mouth.	8	Gently wash baby's bottom. Remove stool and urine from front to back, and use a fresh wipe each time. Dispose directly in designated receptacle.	9	Fold soiled diaper inward and place in designated receptacle followed by the disposable gloves (if used).			
10	Use disposable wipe to clean surface of caregiver's hands and another to clean the child's.	11	Check for spills on paper. If present, fold over so fresh part is under buttocks.	12	Place clean diaper under baby.			
13	Using a cotton ball or tissue, apply skin ointment to clean, dry area if indicated/ordered.	14	Fasten diaper with pins, placing your hand between the child and the diaper on insertion, and dress with fresh clothing.	15	Wash baby's hands with soap and water between 60°F and 120°F for 15–20 sec. and dry. Turn faucet off with a paper towel, then place baby in a safe location.			
16	Clean and disinfect diapering area, leaving bleach solution in contact at least 2 minutes. Allow table to air dry, or wipe it after 2 minutes.	17	Wash your hands with soap and water for at least 15–20 seconds. Turn off faucet with paper towel.	18	Chart diaper change and any observations.			

Adapted from: Standard 3.014 Diaper changing procedure. Caring for our children, National health and safety performance standards (2nd ed.) Used with permission, American Academy of Pediatrics. Permission to photocopy is granted by Thomson Delmar Learning.

Return Practice Demonstration for Disposable Diapering Procedures

Name: _____   Date: _____

Observer: _____

Procedure:

_____   Wash hands with liquid soap and water.

_____   Gather supplies.

_____   Put on disposable waterproof gloves (if used).

_____   Cover diapering surface with nonabsorbent paper liner.

_____   Place baby on prepared diapering area (minimize contact: hold baby away from your body if extremely wet or soiled).

_____   Put soiled clothes in a plastic bag.

_____   Unfasten diaper. Leave soiled diaper under the child.

_____   Gently wash baby's bottom. Remove stool and urine from front to back, and use a fresh wipe each time. Dispose directly in designated receptacle.

_____   Fold soiled diaper inward and place in designated receptacle followed by the disposable gloves (if used).

_____   Use disposable wipe to clean surface of caregiver's hands and another to clean the child's.

_____   Check for spills on paper. If present, fold over so fresh part is under buttocks.

_____   Place clean diaper under baby.

_____   Using a cotton ball or tissue, apply skin ointment to clean, dry area if indicated/ordered.

_____   Fasten diaper and dress with fresh clothing.

_____   Wash baby's hands with soap and water between 60°F and 120°F for 15–20 seconds and dry. Turn faucet off with a paper towel, then place baby in a safe location.

_____   Clean and disinfect diapering area, leaving bleach solution in contact at least 2 minutes. Allow table to air dry, or wipe it after 2 minutes.

_____   Wash your hands with soap and water for at least 15–20 seconds. Turn off faucet with paper towel.

_____   Chart diaper change and any observations.

Return Practice Demonstration for Cloth Diapering Procedures

Name: _____   Date: _____

Observer: _____

Procedure:

_____   Wash hands with liquid soap and water.

_____   Gather supplies.

_____   Put on disposable waterproof gloves (if used).

_____   Cover diapering surface with nonabsorbent paper liner.

_____   Place baby on prepared diapering area (minimize contact: hold baby away from your body if extremely wet or soiled).

_____   Put soiled clothes in a plastic bag.

_____   Unfasten diaper. Leave soiled diaper under the child. Close each safety pin immediately out of child's reach. Never hold pins in mouth.

_____   Gently wash baby's bottom. Remove stool and urine from front to back, and use a fresh wipe each time. Dispose directly in designated receptacle.

_____   Fold soiled diaper inward and place in designated receptacle followed by the disposable gloves (if used).

_____   Use disposable wipe to clean surface of caregiver's hands and another to clean the child's.

_____   Check for spills on paper. If present, fold over so fresh part is under buttocks.

_____   Place clean diaper under baby.

_____   Using a cotton ball or tissue, apply skin ointment to clean, dry area if indicated/ordered.

_____   Fasten diaper with pins, placing your hand between the child and the diaper on insertion, and dress with fresh clothing.

_____   Wash baby's hands with soap and water between 60°F and 120°F for 15–20 seconds and dry. Turn faucet off with a paper towel, then place baby in a safe location.

_____   Clean and disinfect diapering area, leaving bleach solution in contact at least 2 minutes. Allow table to air dry, or wipe it after 2 minutes.

_____   Wash your hands with soap and water for at least 15–20 seconds. Turn off faucet with paper towel.

_____   Chart diaper change and any observations.

Posted Hand Washing Procedures

1	Turn on warm water and adjust to comfortable temperature.	2	Wet hands and apply soap.	3	Wash vigorously for approximately 15–20 seconds.
4	Dry hands with paper towel.	5	Turn off faucet with paper towel.	6	Dispose of paper towel in a lidded trash receptacle with a plastic liner.

Use hand washing procedures for staff and children

- before and after preparing bottles or serving food.
- before and after diapering or toileting.
- before and after administering first aid.
- before and after giving medication.
- before working with the children and at the end of the day.
- before leaving the classroom for a break.
- after wiping nose discharge, coughing, or sneezing.
- before and after playing in the sand and water table.
- after playing with pets.
- after playing outdoors.

Procedure for Cleansing and Sterilizing Bottles, Nipples, Collars and Caps

1. Prewash in hot water with detergent. Scrub the bottles and nipples inside and out with a bottle and nipple brush if necessary. Squeeze water through the nipple hole during the washing procedure.

2. Rinse well with clean hot water.

3. Completely immerse in a bleach solution of 50 parts per million (check with a chlorine strip). Use approximately one-half teaspoon of chlorine bleach to one gallon of water in the final rinse.

4. Bring a large pan of water to a boil, and add one teaspoon of white vinegar to avoid a chalky white buildup. Boil the nipples, collars, and caps for 3 minutes. If bottle liners are not used for the formula, then boil the clean bottles for 5 minutes to sterilize them.

5. Pour the sterilized pieces in a strainer.

6. Air dry thoroughly.

7. Your hands need to be clean and you need to take care in handling techniques to prevent contamination of the clean bottles and nipples.

8. Store the completely dried bottle equipment in a clean, covered, and labeled container away from food items.

Medical Authorization
For Nonprescription Medication*

Name of Child: _____   Date: _____

The staff is authorized to dispense the following medications as ordered by your physician and directed by the parents/guardian.

Please indicate specific medication, route it is to be given, dosage, and frequency.

Type	Medication	Route	Dosage	Frequency
Nonaspirin Preparation				
Aspirin Preparation				
Cough Preparation				
Decongestant				
Skin Ointment				
Diaper Wipes				
Sunscreen				

_____   _____   _____
Print Name of Physician   Signature of Physician   Phone Number

_____
Parent/Guardian Signature

Complete this form on admission and update annually. Store medical authorizations in an index box and place in or near locked cabinet for quick referencing.

Daily Medication Sheet

Child's Name	RX Number & Type of Medication	Amount & Route Administered	Date	Time	Given by:	
					First Name	Last Name

SUGGESTED ILLNESS

Child's name: _____   Date: _____

SYMPTOMS ARE:

_____   Body Temperature (under arm, add 1 degree)

_____   Vomiting

_____   Diarrhea

_____   Exhibiting signs of a communicable illness

_____   Skin condition requiring further treatment

Other: _____

Report initiated by: _____

Were parents notified? Yes _____ No _____ By whom? _____

Time parents notified: 1st Attempt _____

_____
Which Parent Notified

2nd Attempt _____

_____
Which Parent Notified

3rd Attempt _____

_____
Which Parent Notified

Time child departed: _____

Director's signature: _____

Children exhibiting a temperature that exceeds 100°F, symptoms of vomiting (1–3 forceful rushes), diarrhea (defined as watery, mucous, foul-smelling bowel movement) or an unrecognized rash shall not return to group care for a minimum of 24 hours after treatment or before symptoms subside.

1. Office Copy   2. Parent/Guardian Copy

Illness Tracking Reports

Name of Child	Date	Time Called	Type of Illness	Person Reporting Illness	Director Notified	Report Filed	Parent Notified	Time Left

Head Lice Checklist

Group Name: _____

Name	Sunday	Monday	Tuesday	Wednesday	Thursday	Friday	Saturday

C = Clear   **A = Absent**   **P = Possible**

(**Reminder**:   *Please check weekly on different days of the week.*)

Accident/Incident

Child's Name: _____

Date of accident/injury: _____ Time: _____

Brief description of accident/injury: _____

_____

_____

Was first aid given? _____ If so, describe: _____

_____

Was blood present in accident? _____ How much? _____

Were Universal Precautions employed? _____

Was medical intervention required?[*] _____ If yes, describe: _____

_____

Person initiating this report: _____ Witness: _____

Name of parent contacted: _____ Time contacted: _____

Director's signature: _____

In some states it is required to file a copy of this report with the child care licensing department if medical intervention is required.

Accident/Incident Tracking Reports

Name of Child	Date	Time Called	Type of Accident	Person Reporting Accident	Director Notified	Report Filed	Parent Notified	Time Left

SUGGESTED FIRST AID DIRECTIVES

CHOKING

(Conscious) - Stand or kneel behind child with your arms around his waist and make a fist. Place thumb side of fist in the middle of abdomen just above the navel. With moderate pressure, use your other hand to press fist into child's abdomen with a quick, upward thrust. Keep your elbows out and away from child. Repeat thrusts until obstruction is cleared or child begins to cough or becomes unconscious.

(Unconscious) - Position child on his back. Just above navel, place heel of one hand on the midline of abdomen with the other hand placed on top of the first. Using moderate pressure, press into abdomen with a quick, upward thrust. Open airway by tilting head back and lifting chin. **If you can see the object**, do a finger sweep. Slide finger down inside of cheek to base of tongue, sweep object out but be careful not to push the object deeper into the throat. Repeat above until obstruction is removed or child begins coughing. If child does not resume breathing, proceed with artificial respiration (see below).

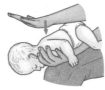

Infants - Support infant's head and neck. Turn infant face down on your forearm. Lower your forearm onto your thigh. Give four (4) back blows forcefully between infant's shoulder blades with heel of hand. Turn infant onto back. Place middle and index fingers on breastbone between nipple line and end of breastbone. Quickly compress breastbone one-half to one inch with each thrust. Repeat backblows and chest thrusts until object is coughed up, infant starts to cry, cough, and breathe, or medical personnel arrives and takes over.

POISONING

Call Poison Control Center (1-800-382-9097) immediately! Have the poison container handy for reference when talking to the center. Do not induce vomiting unless instructed to do so by a health professional. Check the child's airway, breathing, and circulation.

HEMORRHAGING

Use a protective barrier between you and the child (gloves). Then, with a clean pad, apply firm continuous pressure to the bleeding site for five minutes. Do not move/change pads, but you may place additional pads on top of the original one. If bleeding persists, call the doctor or ambulance Open wounds may require a tetanus shot.

SEIZURE

Clear the area around the child of hard or sharp objects. Loosen tight clothing around the neck. Do not restrain the child. Do not force fingers or objects into the child's mouth. After the seizure is over and if the child is not experiencing breathing difficulties, lay him/her on his/her side until he/she regains consciousness or until he/she can be seen by emergency medical personnel. After the seizure, allow the child to rest. Notify parents immediately. If child is experiencing breathing difficulty, or if seizure is lasting longer than 15 minutes, call an ambulance at once.

ARTIFICIAL RESPIRATION *(Rescue Breathing)*

Position child on the back; if not breathing, open airway by gently tilting the head back and lifting chin. Look, listen, and feel for breathing. If still not breathing, keep head tilted back and pinch nose shut. Give two full breaths and then one regular breath every 4 seconds thereafter. Continue for one minute; then look, listen, and feel for the return of breathing. Continue rescue breathing until medical help arrives or breathing resumes.

If using one-way pulmonary resuscitation device, be sure your mouth and child's mouth are sealed around the device.

(Modification for infants only)   Proceed as above, but place your mouth over nose and mouth of the infant. Give light puffs every 3 seconds.

SHOCK

If skin is cold and clammy, as well as face pale or child has nausea or vomiting, or shallow breathing, call for emergency help. Keep the child lying down. Elevate the feet. If there are head/chest injuries, raise the head and shoulders only.

To find your specific
State's Licensing, Rules
and Regulations go to:

http://nrc.uchsc.edu

Emergency Contacts: *Post Near Every Telephone*

Your Facility Address: _____

_____

Nearest Main Intersection: _____

Your Facility Phone Number: _____

Contact	Phone Number
Operator	
Emergency	
Fire	
Police	
Consulting Dentist	
Poison Control	
Local Hospital Emergency Dept	
Other	
Other	

Emergency Evacuation Plan (Template)

Draw First Choice Escape Route, Draw Second Choice Escape Route

Center's Address: _____

Nearest Main Intersection: _____

Center's Phone Number: _____

In Case of Fire Call: _____

In Case of Bomb Threat Call: _____

In Case of Gas Leak Call: _____

Fire Extinguisher Expires Date: _____

Emergency Bag and Blanket Are Located: _____

_____
Place infants in the emergency evacuation beds. If the door is cool, open it slowly, and make sure fire or smoke isn't blocking your escape route. If your escape is blocked, close the door and use an alternative escape route. Smoke and heat rise. Be prepared to crawl where the air is clearer and cooler near the floor. Move as far from the building as possible. In case of a real fire, do not reenter the building until it is cleared by the proper authorities.

Building Evacuation Log

Date	Time of Drill	Evacuation Time	Comments	Full Name of Person in Charge

Tornado Emergency Instructions

Your county or region is: _____

Tornado Watch: A tornado is possible. Remain alert for approaching storms. Tune your portable (battery-operated) radio to a local weather station.

Tornado Warning: A tornado has been sighted. Activate your emergency shelter plan immediately.

Grab your emergency bag and blanket. They are located: _____

_____

Place the infants in the designated emergency evacuation cribs and move calmly and quickly to an interior room or hallway. Account for all children in attendance. Your best location is: _____

_____

Cover cribs with a blanket in case of flying glass or debris.

*Avoid windows, doors, outside walls, and corners of rooms.

Earthquake Emergency Instructions

Prior to earthquakes:
- Brace high and top-heavy objects.
- Fasten cubbies, lockers, toy shelves to the wall.
- Anchor overhead lighting fixtures.
- Install flexible pipe fitting to avoid gas or water leaks.
- Know when and how to shut off electricity, gas, and water at main switches and valves.
- Locate safe spots in the room to protect yourself from dropping debris such as under a sturdy table or crib.

Your safest location is: _____

The shutoff for gas is located: _____

The water main is located: _____

Your emergency bag is located: _____

During an earthquake:

- Stay inside until shaking stops and it is safe to go outside.
- Move the infants to your safe location (inside a crib on an inside wall).
- Place a heavy blanket or lightweight mattress over the crib.
- If you are on the playground, move away from the building.

When the shaking stops be prepared for aftershocks. Check for injuries and administer first aid as indicated. Use flashlights if electricity is out. Do not light candles or matches in case of gas leakage.

Hurricane Emergency Instructions

Hurricane/Tropical Storm Watch: indicates the conditions are expected in the specific are usually within 24 hours.

Hurricane/Tropical Storm Warning: conditions are expected within 24 hours.

Send the children home
Learn your specific evacuation route
Secure your facility
Close storm shutters
Turn utilities off at main valves if instructed by authorities
Take emergency phone numbers with you

Your Evacuation Route: _____

_____

_____

Tornado / Earthquake Drill Log

Date	Time of Drill	Time Needed to Seek Cover	Comments	Full Name of Person in Charge

Infant Receiving Sheet   Date: _____
Welcome, Baby!

Infant's Name	Time Baby Awoke	Last Feeding	Comments, if any	Last Diaper Change

1-3 Months

DEVELOPMENTAL MILESTONES

BABY CAN:

_____   BEGIN TO SMILE AND WILL RESPOND TO SMILING

_____   LOOK AT HANDS

_____   BEGIN TO CONTROL HEAD MOVEMENTS

_____   HOLD A RATTLE BRIEFLY

_____   SQUEAL, COO, & LAUGH

_____   GLANCE FROM ONE THING TO ANOTHER

_____   LIFT HEAD WHEN LYING ON STOMACH

_____   ROLL FROM SIDE TO BACK

_____   RAISE UP ON FOREARMS

_____   BRING OBJECTS TO MOUTH

_____   SIT *SUPPORTED*

_____   TURN HEAD TOWARD VOICES OR SOUNDS

_____   EXPLORE OWN BODY PARTS *(ESP. HANDS & FEET)*

_____   BEGIN TO REACH WITH ACCURACY

Important Note: Infants will develop at similar rates but each in a unique pattern. If you find a baby is not exhibiting the majority of characteristics listed, there could be many plausible reasons ranging from premature birth to a more reserved and cautious personality. This list is a broad overview and not inclusive of all developmental milestones baby will experience.

BABY _____	CAREGIVER _____	DATE _____
Y = YES	S = SOMETIMES	N = NOT YET

4-6 Months

DEVELOPMENTAL MILESTONES

BAGY CAN:

BABY CAN:

_____ BEGIN TO DROOL *(EXCESS SALIVATION AIDS SWALLOWING)*

_____ BEGIN TO SWALLOW SOLIDS

_____ TURN FROM BACK TO SIDE

_____ FOLLOW MOVING OBJECTS WITH EYES

_____ HOLD HEAD ERECT

_____ GURGLE, COO, LAUGH, CRY, & BABBLE

_____ SIT WITH SUPPORT FOR UP TO 30 MINUTES

_____ ROLL FROM BACK TO STOMACH

_____ USE HANDS TO PUT FOOD INTO MOUTH

_____ BEGIN SIGNS OF TEETHING, DROOLING, & CHEWING

_____ MAKE SOUNDS SUCH AS: B, M, D, L, AH, EE, & OO

_____ LOVE REFLECTIONS IN MIRROR

_____ BOUNCE WHEN HELD IN STANDING POSITION

_____ SIT UNSUPPORTED FOR A SHORT TIME

_____ GRAB & PLAY WITH FEET

_____ DRINK FROM A CUP WITH ASSISTANCE

_____ IMITATE SOME SOUNDS YOU MAKE

_____ DROP THINGS ON PURPOSE

_____ ROLL OVER ONTO STOMACH

_____ USE SIMPLE SOUNDS LIKE: BA, MA, DA, PA, GA

> *Important Note: Infants will develop at similar rates but each in a unique pattern. If you find a baby is not exhibiting the majority of characteristics listed, there could be many plausible reasons ranging from premature birth to a more reserved and cautious personality. This list is a broad overview and not inclusive of all developmental milestones baby will experience.*

| BABY _____ | CAREGIVER _____ | DATE _____ |

| Y = YES | S = SOMETIMES | N = NOT YET |

7–9 Months

DEVELOPMENTAL MILESTONES

BABY CAN:

_____ USE FINGERS TO PICK UP OBJECTS

_____ ROCK WHEN ON HANDS AND KNEES

_____ ADOPT ATTACHMENT TO SPECIAL ITEM

_____ ASSUME A SITTING POSITION

_____ PULL UP TO A STANDING POSITION

_____ HOLD TWO SMALL THINGS, ONE IN EACH HAND

_____ EXPERIENCE STRANGER ANXIETY

_____ PICK UP ITEMS AND PUT IN MOUTH

_____ RESPOND TO NAME OR GREETING

_____ BABBLE AS IF SPEAKING A SENTENCE

_____ HOLD A BOTTLE TO DRINK

_____ SCOOT OR CREEP ALONG FLOOR

_____ HAVE GREAT PLEASURE EXPLORING OWN BODY

_____ LOVE TO MAKE NOISE WITH OBJECTS

_____ PICK UP SMALL THINGS W/ THUMB & INDEX FINGER

_____ OFTEN START TO CRAWL

_____ RESPOND TO A FEW SIMPLE DIRECTIONS/REQUESTS

_____ STAND WHEN HAND IS HELD

_____ DRINK FROM A CUP

_____ SHRIEK TO GET ATTENTION

_____ BABBLE, TALK, IMITATE SPEECH SOUNDS

_____ SIT WITHOUT SUPPORT

Important Note: Infants will develop at similar rates but each in a unique pattern. If you find a baby is not exhibiting the majority of characteristics listed, there could be many plausible reasons ranging from premature birth to a more reserved and cautious personality. This list is a broad overview and not inclusive of all developmental milestones baby will experience.

BABY _____	CAREGIVER _____	DATE _____
Y = YES	S = SOMETIMES	N = NOT YET

10-12 Months

DEVELOPMENTAL MILESTONES

BABY CAN:

_____ CRUISE AROUND FURNITURE IN STANDING POSITION

_____ BEGIN TO UNDERSTAND SIMPLE WORDS, DIRECTIVES

_____ BE AFRAID OF LOUD NOISES (*E.G. VACUUM CLEANER*)

_____ START TO MAKE GESTURES (*E.G. BYE-BYE WAVE*)

_____ USE *DA-DA* AND *MA-MA* APPROPRIATELY

_____ CLIMB ON CHAIRS

_____ LOOK AT PICTURES IN A BOOK

_____ PLACE OBJECTS IN A CONTAINER & DUMP OUT

_____ LIFT LIDS OFF OF CONTAINER TO EXPLORE

_____ DROP AND PICK UP OBJECTS

_____ STAND WITHOUT HELP

_____ BABBLE LONG SOUNDS THAT MAY CONTAIN WORDS

_____ ATTEMPT TO ROLL/THROW A BALL BACK TO SOMEONE

_____ USE SIMPLE WORDS: *BALL, DOGGIE, MAMA*

_____ WALK WITH LEGS WIDE APART

_____ PREFER TO CRAWL

_____ STAND UP FROM A SQUATTING POSITION

_____ USE A SPOON BUT *NOT CONSISTENTLY*

_____ COOPERATE WITH GETTING DRESSED

_____ PREFER TO FEED SELF

_____ BEGIN TO SCRIBBLE

_____ FIT ONE THING INTO ANOTHER

> *Important Note: Infants will develop at similar rates but each in a unique pattern. If you find a baby is not exhibiting the majority of characteristics listed, there could be many plausible reasons ranging from premature birth to a more reserved and cautious personality. This list is a broad overview and not inclusive of all developmental milestones baby will experience.*

| BABY _____ | CAREGIVER _____ | DATE _____ |

| Y = YES | S = SOMETIMES | N = NOT YET |

1–3 MONTHS

ALL ACTIVITIES 2–10 MINUTES

Activities to assist baby to build:

Large muscle control • Small muscle control • Language skills
Sensory responses • Mental, cognitive, social growth

THE MUSIC OF SOUND

A SHAKE RATTLE
B PLAY MUSIC OR SING JACK & JILL
C HOLD PUPPET & TALK ABOUT NEW FRIENDS
D SHOW & READ SIMPLE PICTURE BOOK
E WIND UP MUSIC BOX & PLACE NEAR BABY
F TALK TO BABY ABOUT THE SEASON OR WEATHER
G PLACE TOYS NEARBY THAT MAKE SOUNDS BY TOUCH
H PLAY A VARIETY OF MUSIC, MUSIC BOXES, OR MUSICAL TOYS
I SING TWINKLE TWINKLE LITTLE STAR
J SHOW PICTURES OF ANIMALS & TALK ABOUT THEM
K CHOOSE BOOKS REFLECTING BABY'S CULTURAL COMMUNITY

MY BODY IS WONDERFUL

A GENTLY MASSAGE LEGS, ARMS, & BACK
B PLACE ON TUMMY, HOLD TOY A FEW INCHES IN FRONT
C AFTER BABY WRAPS FINGERS AROUND YOUR THUMB, MOVE YOUR HAND FROM SIDE TO SIDE
D GENTLY EXPLORE FACE AND EXTREMETIES WITH COTTON BALL
E ROLL BABY GENTLY ONTO SIDE
F GIVE LARGE TOYS TO BE MOUTHED NOT SWALLOWED
G LAY ON TUMMY & PLACE TOYS WITHIN REACH
H LAY ON BACK & ALLOW BABY TO EXPLORE BODY
I HOLD TOY FOR BABY TO REACH & GRASP
J GENTLY MASSAGE BABY'S FEET AND TOES

MY WORLD

A FEELING YOUR BREATH, BLOW THROUGH A STRAW
B PLACE BABY OVER YOUR SHOULDER, SHOW THE SIGHTS
C PLACE BABY IN FRONT OF MIRROR IN PUMPKIN SEAT
D ROCK BABY IN RHYTHM IN ROCKING CHAIR
E SHINE FLASHLIGHT CIRCLES ABOVE BABY'S HEAD
F ALLOW BABY TO WATCH SELF IN MIRROR
G HOLD BABY UP TO WINDOW, TALK ABOUT WHAT YOU SEE
H USE PUPPET/STUFFED ANIMAL, TALK ABOUT SUN/MOON
I TICKLE BABY'S FACE & HANDS WITH SOFT FABRICS
J SIT BABY SUPPORTED, PLAY W/ BRIGHT COLOR BLOCKS

LIFE IS INTERESTING

A HANG, DISCUSS, PICTURES NEAR DIAPER TABLE, CHANGE OFTEN
B PLACE BABY ON BACK & DANGLE TOY IN FRONT
C PROVIDE A MOBILE OR COLORFUL THINGS TO LOOK AT
D SHOW CARDS OF DIFFERENT COLORS
E GENTLY TOUCH SKIN WITH DIFFERENT SOFT FABRICS
F PLAY PEEKABOO, USE BLANKET, SMILE
G LAY BABY ON BACK, GIVE A TRANSPARENT RATTLE
H GIVE BABY A SOFT RUBBER TOY TO SQUEEZE
I STRING BELLS OVER BABY
J GIVE BABY TOY THAT REFLECTS LIGHT/HAS MIRROR

BABY _____ CAREGIVER _____ DATE _____

4–6 MONTHS

<u>ALL ACTIVITIES 5–10 MINUTES</u>

Activities to assist baby to build:

Large muscle control • Small muscle control • Language skills
Sensory responses • Mental, cognitive, social growth

THE MUSIC OF SOUND

A	MATCH NATURE SOUNDS WITH REAL PICTURES
B	GIVE BABY A TOY THAT SQUEAKS FOR TEETHING
C	PICK A SIMPLE PICTURE BOOK & READ TO BABY
D	SHOW & TALK ABOUT PICTURES OF HOUSEHOLD ITEMS
E	PLAY MUSIC & SING NURSERY RHYMES
F	LISTEN TO RECORDINGS OF BIRD SOUNDS
G	HOLD & SING POP GOES THE WEASEL, LIFT UP ON POP
H	HOLD ON LAP & PLAY PAT-A-CAKE
I	PLAY RECORDED MUSIC FROM MANY CULTURES
J	READ SIMPLE BOOK TO BABY
K	RECITE NURSERY RHYMES OR SIMPLE POETRY
L	READ SIMPLE STORIES USING POP-UP BOOKS
M	PLAY MUSIC WITH STRONG BEAT (E.G. PARADE MUSIC)
N	PLAY PEEKABOO W/SOFT CLOTH, LET BABY PULL OFF
O	SING SONGS, (E.G. HERE WE GO ROUND MULBERRY BUSH)

MY BODY IS WONDERFUL

A	LAY BABY ON BACK, GRASP HANDS & SLOWLY PULL TO SITTING
B	SIT BABY, GENTLY LOWER, REPEAT 6–8 TIMES
C	SIT BABY SUPPORTED, HAND OBJECTS FOR REACHING
D	SIT BABY SUPPORTED, BLOW BUBBLES AROUND BABY
E	HOLD WAIST SECURE, ROLL BACK/FORTH ON BIG BALL
F	SIT ON FLOOR, BABY ON YOUR LEGS TO REACH FOR TOY
G	PUT BABY IN JUMPER SEAT OR BABY BOUNCER
H	PULL BABY BY WAIST TO STAND ON YOUR LAP 3 OR 4 TIMES
I	SIT BABY SUPPORTED, ROLL DIFFERENT BALLS TO BABY
J	LAY ON BACK, GRASP HANDS, SLOW PULL TO SIT & STAND
K	LET BABY GRASP BEADS WHEN CHANGING DIAPER
L	PRACTICE DRINKING SMALL AMOUNTS FROM CUP
M	HAND TOYS BACK & FORTH
N	ALLOW BABY TO PLAY DROP-THE-TOY
O	GIVE 2 OR 3 CUPS THAT FIT INSIDE EACH OTHER

MY WORLD

A	SHOW SEVERAL PICTURES OF HAPPY PEOPLE FACES
B	WALK BABY AROUND ROOM, TALK OF WHAT YOU SEE
C	WALK BABY AROUND ROOM TO TOUCH DIFF. TEXTURES
D	SIT BABY SUPPORTED, GIVE SOFT TOY/ANIMAL TO HUG
E	SHOW FARM ANIMALS & SOUNDS THEY MAKE
F	PUT BABY BY MIRROR TO OBSERVE SELF
G	GIVE A SMALL DAMP WASHCLOTH TO ENJOY
H	SHOW SEVERAL TYPES OF DOG PICTURES
I	GIVE TOYS THAT CREATE NOISES
J	GIVE WASHABLE BRIGHT COLOR PICTURES
K	GIVE SEVERAL TRANSPARENT TOYS TO SEE & DROP
L	GIVE A DISHPAN OF PICTURES
M	GIVE METAL SPOONS IN PAN TO REACH & BANG
N	SIT BABY IN FRONT OF MOUNTED BUSY BOX
O	GIVE STRING OF BIG PLASTIC POP BEADS TO PULL APART

LIFE IS INTERESTING

A	SIT BABY SUPPORTED, ROLL BRIGHT COLORED BALL
B	PLACE BABY ON BACK TO PLAY WITH FLOOR GYM
C	SHOW SEVERAL PICTURES OF DIFFERENT KITTENS
D	TUMMY DOWN, ON BRIGHT COLOR/PATTERN CLOTH/MAT
E	GIVE SEVERAL SIZE RINGS TO HOLD, JIGGLE, CHOMP ON
F	GIVE A VARIETY OF TOYS TO CHEW ON
G	SHOW REAL FLOWERS OR PICTURES
H	BLOW BUBBLES
I	GIVE PAN OF WASHABLE COLOR BLOCKS
J	GIVE SEVERAL RATTLES TO REACH/GRASP
K	PUT DROPS OF WATER IN BABY'S HAND
L	TALK ABOUT PICTURES OF FOOD
M	TALK ABOUT & TOUCH HARD OBJECTS
N	TALK ABOUT & TOUCH SOFT OBJECTS
O	GIVE SMALL WASHABLE BOOKS TO LOOK/CHEW

BABY _____ CAREGIVER _____ DATE _____

7–9 MONTHS

ALL ACTIVITIES 5–10 MINUTES

Activities to assist baby to build:

Large muscle control • Small muscle control • Language skills
Sensory responses • Mental, cognitive, social growth

THE MUSIC OF SOUND

- A READ & SING NURSERY RHYMES
- B PLAY A VARIETY OF MUSIC
- C READ TO BABY FROM BOOK ABOUT BABIES
- D READ ANIMAL BOOKS & IMITATE SOUNDS
- E SING THIS LITTLE PIGGY, USE BABY'S TOES
- F HOW MANY EYES, NOSES, MOUTHS, LEGS, FINGERS
- G SING JACK & JILL
- H PLAY PRE-RECORDED FAMILIAR SOUNDS
- I SING EENSY WEENSY SPIDER
- J SING OLD MCDONALD
- K TALK ABOUT BABY'S TOYS & TEACH THEIR NAMES
- L PUT ITEMS IN PAN, ASK BABY TO CHOOSE EACH ITEM
- M READ VARIETY OF SIMPLE BOOKS WITH REAL PEOPLE FACES
- N HAVE PUPPET TELL BABY ABOUT PUPPET
- O PLAY VARIETY OF MUSIC FROM MANY CULTURES

MY BODY IS WONDERFUL

- A BOUNCE IN BABY BOUNCER
- B HOLD & BOUNCE BABY IN YOUR LAP
- C GIVE COLD TEETHING RINGS TO CHEW ON
- D HOLD BABY'S OUTSTRETCHED ARMS & WALK
- E PLAY PAT-A-CAKE
- F BOUNCE BABY IN LAP TO 1 LITTLE, 2 LITTLE, 3 L... BABIES
- G ROLL DIFFERENT SIZE BALLS TO BABY
- H GENTLY PULL BABY FROM SITTING TO STANDING
- I PUT TOY IN POT WITH LID
- J HELP BABY TO STAND UP TO/DOWN FROM FURNITURE
- K SHOW BABY HOW TO WAVE BYE-BYE
- L SHOW BODY PARTS ON DOLL, THEN ON YOUR BODY
- M SIT ON FLOOR, TOSS TOY, HAVE BABY CRAWL TO GET IT
- N CRAWL WITH BABY, LET BABY PLAY CHASE
- O GIVE ITEMS THAT NEST INSIDE EACH OTHER FOR PLAY

MY WORLD

- A BOUNCE OR ROCK BABY TO UPBEAT MUSIC
- B PLAY PEEKABOO (STILL A FAVORITE)
- C FEED BABY WITH A FUZZY SOCK ON BOTTLE
- D PLAY WITH SCENTED BOTTLES (SEE EQUIP. LIST)
- E PLAY WITH SOAP BUBBLES
- F SHOW DESIGN CARDS, LET BABY EXAMINE CARDS
- G SIT, CRUMBLE PAPER INTO A BALL, LET BABY CRAWL TO IT
- H EXPLORE TEXTURED BOARD BOOKS
- I FILL PAN W/ 2" CUBES FOR BABY TO PLAY WITH
- J GIVE BABY SOFT DOLLS TO PLAY WITH
- K PLAY COPYCAT, BANG SPOON, PAT/TIP HEAD SIDE TO SIDE
- L COLOR W/ 1 FAT CRAYON, TAPE PAPER TO HIGHCHAIR TRAY
- M SIT & SHOW BABY HOW TO STACK LARGE BLOCKS
- N SIT BABY BY MIRROR & TRY ON DIFFERENT HATS
- O GIVE PURSE WITH FUN OBJECTS TO EXPLORE

LIFE IS INTERESTING

- A DANCE WITH BABY
- B LISTEN TO TICK TOCK ON WOUND-UP CLOCK
- C LISTEN TO SOUNDS ON BIG BLANKET OUTSIDE
- D LAY BABY ON DIFFERENT TEXTURE RUGS TO CRAWL
- E TICKLE BABY WITH A FEATHER
- F EXPLORE CONTRASTS PROVIDE WARM & COOL WASHCLOTHS
- G PUT CLEAN SAFE SIZE ROCKS IN PAN TO EMPTY/FILL
- H PLAY WITH TOY TELEPHONE
- I PLAY HIDE & SEEK UNDER BLANKET W/ FAMILIAR TOY
- J LOOK AT PICTURES OF NATURE
- K SWING IN OUTDOOR BABY SWING
- L GIVE BABY PANS, LIDS, LARGE PLASTIC SPOONS
- M SHOW HOW TO ROCK, PAT, & HUG DOLL
- N SHOW PICTURES OF PEOPLE BUSY AT WORK/PLAY
- O SHOW HOW TO FEED A DOLL

BABY _____ CAREGIVER _____ DATE _____ .

Permission to photocopy is granted by Thomson Delmar Learning.

10-12 MONTHS

ALL ACTIVITIES 5-20 MINUTES

Activities to assist baby build:

Large muscle control • Small muscle control • Language skills
Sensory responses • Mental, Cognitive • Social Growth

	THE MUSIC OF SOUND
A	ECHO BABY'S SOUNDS & BABBLE BACK TO BABY
B	TIE CANNING JAR LIDS TOGETHER FOR BABY TO SHAKE
C	READ & LET BABY TURN PAGES OF BOOK
D	LET BABY WATCH, LISTEN, TAKE PART IN PUPPET PLAY
E	PLAY PARADE, GIVE BABY SPOON & PAN TO BEAT
F	CLAP HANDS TO THE MUSIC BEAT
G	LOOK AT PICTURE BOOKS WITH EVERYDAY ITEMS
H	REPEAT BABY'S WORDS
I	GIVE A VARIETY OF BELLS TO RING
J	PLAY MUSIC TO MATCH BABY'S MOOD
K	GIVE EASY-TO-PLAY MUSIC TOY
L	READ BOOKS THAT TELL SIMPLE STORIES
M	PLAY MUSICAL INSTRUMENTS
N	LOOK AT WORD BOOK WITH MATCHING PICTURES
O	SING THE WHEELS ON THE BUS

	MY BODY IS WONDERFUL
A	GENTLY MASSAGE BABY'S FEET & LEGS
B	GENTLY ROLL BABY OVER LARGE BEACH BALL
C	PLAY PAT-A-CAKE, HAVE BABY PLAY BACK/CLAP
D	HAND UP TO 3 SMALL TOYS TO BABY TO GRASP
E	ACT OUT POP GOES THE WEASEL
F	CRAWL BEHIND BABY, PLAY CATCH ME
G	SHOW HOW TO CRAWL & PUSH A TOY CAR
H	PUSH OR RIDE ON PLAY CAR
I	SHOW HOW TO REMOVE RINGS FROM STACKING TOY
J	GIVE PAN OF COASTERS OR CANNING RINGS
K	GIVE LARGE DUPLO BLOCKS TO PUT TOGETHER
L	SHOW HOW TO USE SIMPLE SORTER
M	SHOW HOW TO PUSH LAWN MOWER/CORN POPPER
N	GIVE PULL TOY
O	GIVE PUSH CART FULL OF DISHES

	MY WORLD
A	HAVE BABY DUMP BLOCKS, REMOVE ONE AT A TIME
B	PRACTICE STACKING ITEMS
C	GIVE BABY A CLEAN WHISK BROOM TO EXPLORE
D	SHOW BABY HOW TO PLAY TOY PIANO/XYLOPHONE
E	GIVE BABY MILK JUG TO RATTLE & SHAKE
F	PLAY PEAK-A-BOO, BABY COVERS OWN EYES
G	GIVE LARGE NESTING CUPS FOR PLAY
H	GIVE PLASTIC BABY KEYS
I	GIVE A PAN W/LID FULL OF FUN ITEMS
J	GIVE A CAN OF TENNIS BALLS
K	MAKE STICKY BALLS OF WADDED TAPE TO EXPLORE
L	PLAY TEDDY-BEAR, TEDDY-BEAR
M	LAY ON FLOOR, LET BABY CLIMB ON YOU
N	BOUNCE BABY ON LAP, SING TEN LITTLE INDIANS
O	PLAY WITH BALLS

	LIFE IS INTERESTING
A	HIDE A TOY UNDER BLANKET FOR BABY TO FIND
B	HOLD BABY, PLAY RING AROUND THE ROSY
C	SHOW PICTURES OF ANIMALS & PRACTICE SOUNDS
D	SHOW HOW TO COVER & ROCK DOLL TO SLEEP
E	SIT BY MIRROR, SING ABOUT NOSE, EYES, EARS, MOUTH, HAIR. USE THE TUNE HERE WE GO 'ROUND THE
F	MULBERRY BUSH
G	SHOW PICTURES OF FOOD
H	SHOW PICTURES OF CLOTHES
I	SHOW HOW ITEMS MATCH IN COLOR, SIZE, SHAPE...ETC.
J	DROP CLOTHES PINS IN MILK JUG... NO SPRINGS
K	BLOW SOAP BUBBLES FOR BABY
L	PLAY DRESS UP
M	PLAY ON SIMPLE SLIDE
N	STACK FIRM PILLOWS TO CLIMB ON
O	SHOW PICTURES OF MODES OF TRANSPORTATION

BABY _____ CARETEACHER _____ DATE _____

PERSONAL SUPPLY INVENTORY CHECKLIST

INFANT'S NAME: _____ **DATE:** _____

SUPPLY	FULL	HALF	NEED MORE
Diapers			
Disposable wipes			
Waterproof paper for diaper barrier (such as wax paper)			
Diaper ointment			
Clothing			
Pacifier/pacifier safety clip			
Bottles			
Nipples			
Bottle liners			
Jarred food			
Baby cereal			
Other:			

To find your specific
State's Licensing, Rules
and Regulations go to:

http://nrc.uchsc.edu

APPENDIX

Gloving

B

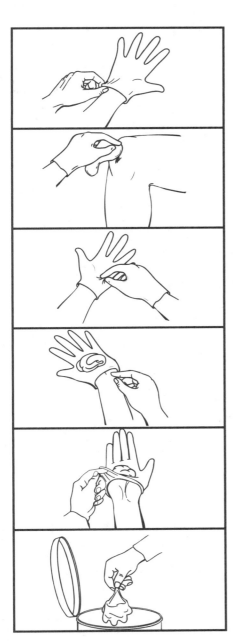

Put on a clean pair of gloves.

Provide the appropriate care.

Remove each glove carefully. Grab the first glove at the palm and strip the glove off. Touch dirty surfaces only to dirty surfaces.

Ball-up the dirty glove in the palm of the other gloved hand.

With the clean hand strip the glove off from underneath at the wrist, turning the glove inside out. Touch dirty surfaces only to dirty surfaces.

Discard the dirty gloves immediately in a step can. Wash your hands.

Reference: California Department of Education. *Keeping Kids Healthy: Preventing and Managing Communicable Disease in Child Care.* Sacramento, CA: California Department of Education, 1995.

To find your specific
State's Licensing, Rules
and Regulations go to:

http://nrc.uchsc.edu

Washing Hands

1) Wet hands.

2) Add soap.

3) Rub hands together.

4) Rinse hands with fingers down.

5) Dry your hands with a towel.

6) Turn off water with paper towel.

7) Toss the paper towel in the trash.

Good Job!

Reprinted with permission from the National Association of Child Care Professionals, http://www.naccp.org.